# THE ECHOLS FILES

## CATOOSA COUNTY JUSTICE

### A TRUE-LIFE ACCOUNT FROM THE
### PRIVATE INVESTIGATOR'S PERSPECTIVE

## BY ERIC D. ECHOLS, CFI

Cover design by Duane Crockett, Crockett Design
Editing by Zuzana Urbanek and Susan Barrows
Interior layout by Zuzana Urbanek, Z-ink.net

Printed in the United States of America


Library of Congress Cataloging-in-Publication Data

Echols, Eric D.
    The Echols files: Catoosa County justice / Eric D. Echols
    ISBN-10  0615634028
    ISBN-13  978-0615634029
    1. Memoirs. 2. Social Services & Welfare, Criminology.

# Acknowledgements

Thanks to my lovely wife Patricia, my loving children Erica, Ryan, Shelby and Sydney. Thanks to my family and friends who have supported me throughout this crisis in my life. Thanks to those who have shown me the way and those I have learned from. Thanks to Detroit for giving me my background and the US Marines for giving me my structure. Thanks to the private investigators that have supported me and to the people in Catoosa County who have made this book a wakeup call. Most importantly, thanks to GOD for ALL the blessings you have bestowed upon me and my family!

# TABLE OF CONTENTS

# PREFACE

This book is meant to let people know that there are areas where injustice still occurs, where favoritism, back alley dealings, rulings and decisions are made solely by the social class of a person, financial influences, or the color of skin. You will be astonished at the facts that were identified in the investigation of The State of Georgia vs. Tonya Henke Craft. Tonya was a school teacher at Chickamauga Elementary and was charged with molesting three little girls, one of which was Tonya's own daughter. Reading this book you will go through the investigation and read about what evidence was found and why I was falsely arrested and charged with three felony counts of witness influencing by the district attorney in Catoosa County.

After reading this book you will be embarrassed to say you live in a country where justice is really Just – Us. Us... meaning for those that are well connected, wealthy, and should be protecting the law. This book will be a guide to those in the field of private investigations working national news child molestation cases. It will also provide light to attorney's that have a client who has been falsely accused of child molestation, which is the most horrific and appalling of crimes.

As the lead private investigator in the Craft case, I personally conducted the investigation and seen how the story of Tonya Craft was validated throughout my investigation as one of the biggest conspiracies involving state agencies, the district attorney's office and the Sheriff Department in Catoosa County Georgia. Now it's time to expose those individuals in Catoosa County and let them know that all people are created equal.

# About the Author

Eric D. Echols born in Detroit, Michigan is the Co-Founder, President and CEO of The LPS Group, Inc. The LPS Group is a privately owned loss prevention, private detective and security corporation that works closely with their clients to prevent losses while increasing their revenue, provide confidential investigation, surveillance, personal protection and property protection. The LPS Group, Inc. was formed in September 2003 by Eric D. Echols for the purpose of providing true loss prevention, private investigations, and security services with honesty and integrity.

Eric has more than twenty five years of experience in loss prevention and investigations where he held executive positions for many years (e.g., Divisional Vice President of Loss Prevention, Regional Director of Loss Prevention, Manager of Investigations and Director of Loss Prevention). Eric also served in the United States Marine Corps as Corporal in the Military Police (Barracks Duty) and in the Fleet Marine Force (Infantry), while in the Marine Corps Eric received recognition for outstanding performance and was awarded three meritorious mast, two letters of appreciation, and the Good Conduct Ribbon. Eric has extensive security experience in retail, hotel, and corporate industries. Eric is a Certified Forensic Interviewer (CFI) and has interview and interrogation experience in retail, criminal, and civil investigations. Eric is a Licensed Private Investigator in Georgia,

Tennessee and North Carolina; an Instructor, and Firearms Trainer for the State of Georgia through the Secretary of State, Private Detective and Security Agencies. Eric's experience and knowledge in criminal and civil investigations, employee theft, premises liability, and security negligence makes him one of the best in the field of private investigations.

Eric D. Echols, CFI
1050 E. Piedmont Road, Suite E-134
Marietta, GA 30062
eric@lpsgroup.net
(770) 579-0188

# THE ECHOLS FILES

## CATOOSA COUNTY JUSTICE

A TRUE-LIFE ACCOUNT FROM THE
PRIVATE INVESTIGATOR'S PERSPECTIVE

BY ERIC D. ECHOLS, CFI

# FOREWORD

*Will it ever change?*

This question has been asked throughout history. Every time there is an injustice and someone, any human being, suffers a violation of his or her constitutional rights, the question arises: "Will it ever change?"

Our primary constitutional right is the freedom we are granted. It's the freedom our grandfathers and forefathers fought for; it's the freedom we, being Americans, hold true. And this freedom cannot be denied by anyone—not the government, or those politicians we voted into office, or those whom they hire. Because after all, this is the United States of America. Every time another injustice is committed or someone's civil liberties are withheld, the question resounds: "Will it ever change?" Civil liberties are a crucial privilege to Americans; our civil liberties are our rights and freedoms that protect us, the "We the People" written in the Constitution. These guaranteed rights stand between each of us and those who try to take away our liberties and violate them— which includes our own government. These liberties set boundaries so that even people within the government cannot abuse their power and interfere improperly with the lives of private citizens—"We the People."

The guidelines are all written out, plain as day, in our country's documents. The Declaration of Independence states, "We hold these truths to be self-evident, that all men are created equal, that they are endowed by their Creator with certain unalienable Rights, that among these are Life, Liberty and the pursuit of Happiness." Basically this means that God created all humans to be equal and in doing so, God blessed everyone with life, the freedom to think or act free from constraint or force, and the talents to be prosperous and happy. And because these are blessings from God, they cannot be surrendered to or taken by anyone.

But there are those who see these beautiful, God-given rights as something to be leveraged. Unfortunately, I know this first-hand. All too often, the element that fires some horrific act of injustice is an otherwise insignificant detail, nothing more than a stray word, a mistaken tone—or a disliked color. When we're talking about the color of a person's skin—well, even in this supposedly enlightened day and age, that minor detail can be a lightning rod that triggers a whole shock wave of deep, dark denial … *generations* of it. That was the ugly harvest my investigation reaped.

So when you look at how people are put into classes based on financial and social status, or how people mistreat others, violate them as humans, and take away their rights for no reason other than that they can, it all seems senseless! The Tonya Craft case made me think about my liberties and those of others. What happened in this case shook me to my core; it humbled me, and made me look at the ways I deal with people. It even affected how my company conducts its business.

The Tonya Craft case and others like it will always make me wonder if that nagging question "Will it ever change?" will eventually one day be answered—and if then, whether we will have the merest ghost of a chance that the answer will be "YES, IT WILL!"

*Eric D. Echols, CFI*
*Private Investigator*

# Ringgold, Georgia

April 2011, you could trace the tornado had taken by the shattered destruction it had left in its path

The little town of Ringgold in Catoosa County, Georgia, is the stereotypical sleepy little Southern town, a blip on the map that to most people means little more than a last Georgia gas stop on I-75 as it snakes toward the Tennessee border. The interstate highway weaves its way up through wooded, hilly country, the thick stands of pine trees permitting only a brief glimpse of the town of Ringgold.

Now Ringgold was no longer shielded from the outside world. The tornado's swath had left a visible gash across the rolling, forested hills, and now the town lay exposed, and ravaged. The twister had come clean across Exit 348 as if it were tooling down Old Alabama Road, taking out acres of old-growth pines and everything else in its way. The homes situated on top of the hill west of the exit had had a spectacular view the tranquil landscape, but now the view was of breathtaking destruction—at least, it would have been a view for somebody if the houses were still intact. Trees had been uprooted and tossed like toothpicks. The ones still standing were snapped off and splintered, their naked limbs stripped of leaves. Clumps of soggy insulation clung to the broken-off trees like Spanish moss, and broken glass and twisted sheet metal littered the ground. But it seemed as though nature had saved its full wrath for Ringgold's main commercial strip of motels and fast-food chains. A dozen highway-friendly signs on towering pylons were now just high, crooked poles with battered, empty metal boxes on top.

As I drove through Ringgold and saw these scenes, I couldn't help but think that this was meaningful. It was as if the tornado's destruction was a physical manifestation of the painful events that had happened there just a couple of years before—events that had threatened to rip open the very soul of Ringgold, making victims of its citizens, the good and the evil alike.

I know all about it, all the nasty details. Lucky me—I was in the middle of it all. And to tell you the God's honest truth, I'd rather have had to deal with the tornado. A tornado can kill—but it doesn't actively, mindlessly *hate*.

If there's one thing I despise, is hate.

# Mrs. Tonya Henke Craft — The Meeting

To understand the story I'm about to tell, it's good to know where I'm coming from. I'm a private investigator, a hard working one, I might add, because I take pride in my work. But I'm not just a cold, investigating machine. I'm as human as they come, and I'm hanging on to my humanity throughout this story, so you'll have to excuse me as I indulge in a few segues along the way.

For instance, I love movies, and I have all my life. So many times something I'm going through brings to mind something I've seen before in a film. Seeing art reflected in life helps add a bit of color to the mundane day-to-day routine. The funny thing is that sometimes events in my life play out in exactly the same ways I've seen on the screen.

Catoosa County was like a movie, but far from a comedy. It was like being in one of those '70s drive-in movies. You know the kind I mean—one of those cheesy exploitation movies where some backwater Southern town is run by a corrupt justice system, and the judge, prosecutor, and sheriff all have one thing in common: their own kind of justice. Or one of those movies in which someone high up in the small-town social order makes the rules, and the authorities in that town do whatever the well-known, wealthy, or connected one wants done and to whomever they want it done to. Movies like *Walking Tall*, *Brubaker*, *In the Heat of the Night*, or

*Road House* immediately come to mind. Or any one of the movies showing someone who's been framed, arrested, and even incarcerated for a crime they did not commit—like *The Hurricane*, the true story about Rubin "Hurricane" Carter, who was unjustly framed for murder or one of best movies I have ever seen, *The Shawshank Redemption*.

I would watch movies like these when I was growing up, and then later with my children —and I would find myself wondering, "Could this be true?" or "Does that attitude still exist?" These were the kinds of movies I watched as a young African American, growing up in Detroit, Michigan, living in an all-black community. The only whites I ever knew were the characters I saw on the TV or movie screen. In these movies, African Americans were often depicted as being afraid of standing up to whites, especially those African Americans in the South. This was an unfortunate fact of life from the time my grandparents were children—and, regrettably, it's still true up until now in some areas.

Finally, I came of age and left my comfort zone. To say my comfort zone was Detroit, Michigan tells a lot about me. I set out to see what the world had to offer and to make my mark in society and become a man. I accomplished this by joining the finest fighting organization in the world. I'm talking about a branch of the service that instills bravery, honor, *esprit de corps*—a branch of the service that trains you how to kill and do it quickly and effectively, a branch of the service that teaches you how to "kick ass and take names." I'm talking about the United States Marine Corps. The Corps embedded that "kick ass" philosophy in my way of thinking and in everything I do. And just so you know, "Once a Marine, always a Marine!"

In retrospect, the USMC taught me how to deal with those old ideologies of the South. The Corps instilled in me the will to deal and the need to succeed, which means you deal with any adversities and succeed professionally in any mission set before you. And that training would serve me in good stead—damned good stead. Because those old ideologies that I had thought long gone were not; they were just hidden. And we all know—a truth that is hidden always, *always* finds a way out.

So come along with me as I take you through two years of my life, from 2008 to 2010, as I worked on a criminal case that shook me and many others to our foundations. This case will reveal to America that in a small town called Ringgold in Catoosa County, Georgia, there were still some of the antiquated Southern ideologies at work in the county government and the judicial system, those traditional under-the-table methods of operation used by those who regarded themselves as influential and well connected. Since the case broke, those who thought they ran the Catoosa County justice system finally have hard evidence before them that they don't. Of course, it remains to be seen if this whole horrible incident will change their ways—but operating in the shadows becomes difficult with the full light of the truth shining bright.

That's why I'm going to tell you about the case of *The State of Georgia vs. Tonya Henke Craft.*

It all started on Wednesday, July 30, 2008, at 9:30 a.m., when I arrived at the law offices of Slater & King on Peachtree Street in downtown Atlanta, Georgia. Slater & King at this time had already been clients of the LPS Group, Inc., a loss-prevention, private investigations, security corporation that my wife Patricia and I own. When I arrived at their office, I was taken to the conference room. In the conference room sat Scott and Cary King, the father-and-son team of Slater & King. Also in the room was a slim, blond-haired lady about five-foot-four. She was hard not to notice—she looked for all the world like a blond Dixie Carter from the TV show *Designing Women*. She was just chattering away in an eloquent Julia Sugarbaker voice that had a soft Southern twang. She seemed to be a pleasant person, outspoken, self-assured, and sassy, full of spunk. Her personality and looks drew so much attention that the somber man in the dark suit sitting next to her almost seemed to be in her shadow. When the introductions were made, I found out the blond woman's name was Mrs. Tonya Henke Craft. The man in the suit was her attorney, Clancy Covert of the Luther-Anderson Law Firm out of Chattanooga, Tennessee. Not knowing what the case was going to be about, my first thought was that this lady must be stuck in the middle of yet another garden-variety domestic case involving either infidelity or child custody. But I reminded myself that in this business of private investigations, you stay professional and always keep an open mind, because you never know what type of case you are going to get.

Good thing I was prepared, because in the next breath, I was informed it was a criminal case—and, more specifically, a child molestation case. When I heard the type of case, my poker face almost failed me. I sat down, took out my notepad, and said, "OK, I'm listening." Over the next three hours, I was through the looking glass. Tonya, her voice sometimes breaking, did most of the talking, with details added by the phalanx of lawyers. Even while she was obviously upset, I noted that she was trying to state matters as objectively as she could. Her answers were forthcoming and direct, and she seemed to be free of arrogance and conceit, two factors that always present obstacles to uncovering the full story about something. And as for stories, Tonya Craft's was already shaping up into one I had never before encountered.

As I filled my notebook with the details, I couldn't help but shake my head. This was one of the most unusual child molestation cases I had ever heard. The defendant was a female, and the alleged victims were all female girls of five and six years of age. Now, in all the child molestation cases I was familiar with where the defendants were female, the alleged victims had been boys—in most cases, teenage boys. I have heard about male defendants where the alleged victims were little boys, the sad situation you hear about all too frequently in the media. But a case where the defendant was female with little girls as the alleged victims was off the charts, at least to me. It was so uncommon that I was intrigued from the start. I told Tonya to just relax, and tell me her story in the order in which she experienced it.

Her side of the story went as follows: Tonya Craft was a kindergarten teacher at Chickamauga Elementary School in Ringgold, Georgia. When it was time to assess each student's progress before passing up to the next grade level, Tonya did not feel that a particular child was ready to move up. This was the daughter of Walter DeWayne and Sherry D. Wilson. When they received the news, the irate Wilsons called the principal and demanded a meeting with Tonya at the school to discuss the situation with their daughter. Tonya had expected some ruffled feathers over her verdict, but at the meeting, she was met with full-on rage from the parents. Mr. Wilson was beyond being reasoned with; he told Tonya that she was not going to embarrass him or his family by not passing his daughter. Tonya explained to me that when she said she could not pass his daughter, Mr. Wilson "got very upset and told me that I was not going to embarrass his family and he would get me"

Tonya then began to tell me of an incident that occurred at the Wilsons' home. It was there that the children of Jerry and Kelli McDonald, Greg and Sandra Lamb, and Joey and Kim Walker were playing with the Wilsons' daughter. The children had been drawing with chalk on the sidewalk out in front of the Wilson house. Afterward, something written among the scribbled drawings caught the eye of one of the parents. There on the sidewalk, in a childish scrawl, was the word "sex."

By the time the word was discovered, the children's games had taken them away from the sidewalk and across the yard. It was not clear which child had written the word; however, the incident rattled the parents enough to get them to talking about how children five and six years old knew the word "sex" and how to write it out.

Then, to my surprise, Tonya brought up the fact that previously there had been a disturbing incident that had involved her very own daughter. She had suspicions that her five-year-old girl had been a victim of inappropriate sexual behavior involving her ex-husband's new wife, Sarah Bass Henke. At the time, the daughter was in the full custody of her natural mother, Tonya Craft, but Joal Henke her ex-husband had visitation rights. According to Tonya, her daughter came back from a visitation at her father's house and told her mother about an odd situation that had occurred there. The child had been invited to take a shower with Sarah Henke and, while in the shower, Sarah had shown the little girl how she shaved her pubic hair. Hearing this, my first thought was, "What the hell is a stepmother doing, showering with a stepdaughter in a new marriage?" Then I tried to figure out why a stepmother would show a five-year-old how to shave her pubes she did not have. This had allegedly happened on more than one occasion. Tonya stated she was so concerned, she contacted authorities in Tennessee and lodged a complaint with Family Services to open an investigation.

Tonya's story then led to an incident regarding her daughter's birthday party. It was held at Tonya's house, for her daughter. Among the guests were the daughters of Jerry and Kelli McDonald, Greg and Sandra Lamb, and Joey and Kim Walker and others. At one point during the party, the Lamb and McDonald girls were being mean to Tonya's daughter. When she noticed how those two girls were treating her daughter, Tonya told the two children that they were being mean and to stop. The Lamb girl got upset and contacted her mother, Sandra Lamb, who shortly pulled up in Tonya's driveway just long enough to pick up her daughter and the McDonald girl. Sandra didn't say a word to Tonya; she ushered the girls into her SUV without inquiring as to what happened and drove off in a huff.

There seemed to be a high degree of social friction between Tonya and these three families in particular. She explained how she had had a few other awkward and heated misunderstandings and overreactions with them—all incidents that led up to these allegations. I had to ask Tonya if there were any incidents of her own where her behavior with any of the alleged victims could be construed as touching. Tonya then informed me about a situation when her very own daughter was not feeling well and had a rash or something on her bottom. Tonya stated that she put medication on her daughter's bottom to ease the pain. Tonya then added she didn't do anything out of the norm that any other mother wouldn't do for their child who had a similar rash.

Tonya then began to talk about a weird game she knew about, as well as all the parents knew that all the children would play. This game was played by the children of Tonya, the Lambs, the Walkers, the Wilsons, and the McDonalds. The game was called the "boyfriend-girlfriend game," and the children would act out being boyfriends and girlfriends. There was even a situation during the game in which the McDonald girl and Tonya's daughter had explored each other's private parts. This was witnessed by one of the parents and widely reported by them. When I first heard about this game, my first thought was that all the parents who knew of this game should have put a stop to it. But I reminded myself again I was being told about a case and that personal feelings were to be left out. Nevertheless this bizarre game had been permitted by the parents. They all knew about this game, and there were times the parents even watched the kids play it.

Tonya then explained to me that Sandra Lamb came from a wealthy family; she benefited personally from that wealth. Sandra's father owned two businesses where Sandra was employed (or just drew a check). Sandra's husband, Greg, was an executive officer working for the same company. Tonya even added that the Lambs daughter is a child actress who has been on the big screen (in the 2008 film *One Missed Call*). Tonya further explained that the Lambs were well connected politically to the offices of the district attorney and the sheriff in Catoosa County, Georgia, and had ties to Mr. Bobby Lee Cook, attorney at law. Now just about every attorney in Georgia and maybe in the nation has heard of Bobby Lee Cook. If you have not heard of Mr. Cook, just turn on TV Land and watch the old episodes of *Matlock*. You see, the character of Ben Matlock was based on the celebrated law career of Mr. Bobby Lee Cook. So let's just say the Lambs were connected.

Now, the combined effect of the incident at the birthday party, the writing of "sex" on the sidewalk, and the two little girls touching each other's privates ignited a firestorm of reaction. Gossip was repeated and phone calls were flying between Sandra Lamb, Kelly McDonald, and Sherry Wilson. Even Tonya's ex-husband Joal Henke got drawn into the witch-hunt.

Remember when you were a child and you told someone a story? Well, by the time the story got back to you it was changed, embellished, and twisted into something wildly different from the story you began with. Now, picture that this particular story started off with someone making the whole thing up from the beginning. Just imagine how the compounded hysteria—taking what was basically an incident of child-on-child sexual experimentation and tempering it with high degrees of personal psychological denial—could turn into finger pointing accusations of Tonya having herself committed acts of child molestation. By the time Sandra Lamb, Kelly McDonald, and Sherry Wilson finished working their phones, the Catoosa County sheriff was on Tonya Craft's front step.

Tonya was arrested, charged with twenty-two (22) crimes, including ten (10) counts of child molestation, six (6) counts of aggravated sexual battery, and six (6) counts of aggravated child molestation. It was possible for her to receive 440 years in prison; that's just another way of saying LIFE.

Back in the Slater & King offices, I put down my pen, rocked back in my chair, and rubbed my eyes. So *this* was the story. To myself I was saying, "WOW! What a story!" But private investigators, if they are good, will not make decisions based solely on what the client has told them. This type of thinking impedes the investigation and taints the objectivity of the facts and information found during the investigation. As to Tonya Craft's innocence or guilt, I wasn't making any bets this early in the investigation. It was not until much later when I was well into my investigation that I started believing her version of events. But from the start, the details of her story were so compelling that I really wanted to ferret out the truth behind this whole ugly situation.

As I was being told this story and other facts of the case, I was jotting down the thoughts that came to my mind. The questions I ask in an investigation are my most important tools; the right questions make all the difference, because sometimes in a complex case, you can't arrive at the real, total answers without them. In a case, I'm dealing with a situation that has already occurred and sometimes is long over. It's the nature of my business, and I'm lucky to have abilities that give me an advantage in this area. I need that edge, because sometimes actual physical evidence is lacking or nonexistent, and I have nothing to get at the truth with but intangible things like the memories of other people. Coming along after the fact, I have to understand as exactly as humanly possible how a sequence of events happened. An event might be totally real and factual, but reality gets filtered through each person's perceptions differently. I have to take the evidence and answers I get, weigh the merits and believability of each, and use them as building blocks to recreate the situation in my mind. Asking the right questions gives me the answers I'm looking for to fill in the gaps on the whole picture.

Tonya finished her story and sat back in her chair, apparently relieved to stop talking about her case for a moment. "Sorry, ma'am," I told her, "Now I have some questions" She smiled a weary smile and sat forward again, ready to face my music. Here was my first chance to see what more I could find out. I carefully looked for telltale changes in her body language or tone of voice as I asked her the following questions:

1. Why do you think this is happening to you?
2. Who initially reported these alleged incidents?
3. Who are the key players in this case, and what was your relationship to them?
4. What type of people are they?
5. What information do you have that supports what you are telling me?
6. What type of person are you?
7. What will people say about you?
8. Have you ever been in trouble prior to these allegations?
9. Where is your current husband in this, and is he supportive of you?
10. Is there anything I need to know that you have not told me?

Note that the subjective questions— numbers 1, 4, and 6—are like barometers. They measure the intangibles like feelings and perceptions and allow me to get a feel for possible motives involved. As for Tonya's body language, I couldn't detect any postures or twitches that indicated deceit. She was direct and non-evasive. When my questions touched on intimately personal subjects, she looked me straight in the eyes and answered the questions. As for the precise answers, I'll get back to those shortly. I wrote down Tonya Craft's answers and my own observations with a feeling in the back of my mind that this whole thing was going to wind up being bigger than it seemed at first glance. Believe me, I had many more questions during this first meeting with Tonya and her attorneys, our clients.

Over the following long months, a continual flurry of questions, conversations, and meetings became routine with Tonya. Often in an investigation, the client will be asked the same questions over and over in an attempt to elicit some small, previously unmentioned bit of evidence which might have bearing on the case, and Tonya's situation was certainly no exception. Again and again I took her through each stage of the events; I asked her the same questions so many times that I didn't have to look at my notes. And through it all, she endured my endless interrogations like a trooper. Picture yourself in the same position: imagine you've been charged with twenty-two felony counts of child molestation, and think to yourself—how much could *you* take?

But that is just a glimpse into the future of this case. I was talking about my first meeting with Tonya Craft.

For an initial discussion, it was full of leads and incidents to check out. As I had listened to Tonya's story unfold, it outlined to me a possible scenario where she was being made the victim of a conspiracy and a cover up, but again it was too soon to hang my hat on this scenario. I asked a few remaining questions and then we wrapped it up for the day. Everyone stood up to leave, groaning at their cramped legs from the three-hour sit-down. I closed my notebook, slid my pen in my jacket pocket, and shook hands all around with the attorneys. Then I turned to Tonya. As I shook her hand, I paused and looked her straight in the eye. I told her, "I will investigate you and this case thoroughly—and if the truth reveals you are in fact guilty, I will find that out as well."

She didn't flinch... She did however look at me with a slight grin and shook her head in agreement. I like that in a client. I know well that later Tonya vividly remembered me telling her this—all because of the *Catoosa County News*. In an article that was written up on February 10, 2011, Tonya, in her distinctively forthright way, repeated the incident to a reporter:

*"Eric was very up front from the very beginning," she said. "He told me from day one that if in his investigation he uncovered that I was in fact guilty of the charges I was facing, that whatever he found would become public knowledge and that the truth would be exposed. I accepted that guarantee from him, because I knew that I hadn't committed the crimes I was being accused of."*

# THE INVESTIGATION BEGINS

After the meeting with Tonya and the attorneys, I went back to my office in Marietta, Georgia. During the drive back, all I thought about was the story I had been told and what I could bring to the table as the private investigator assigned to this case to aid in the defense of Tonya. When I arrived back at my office, I pulled the staff together and explained the case to them all. Involving everyone from the get-go was not standard operating procedure at The LPS Group. Typically I just meet privately with a client to discuss the case, any options they have, and whether my terms, both monetary and ethical, are agreeable—then I begin the work or assign parts of the case to my investigators. But this case was different, different on so many levels: the people involved, the who's who; the area where the alleged crimes took place; the racial makeup of our firm and of those people who were involved; the multitude of charges, the disturbing nature of the charges, and so on.

About the charges, let me say this:

I knew what child molestation was—a crude sexual act or sexual acts with a minor under fourteen years old. But to get the full scope of the crimes for which Tonya was being charged and arrested for, I had to look them up—and what I learned about this crime turned even my Marine's guts. I certainly knew that this evil existed. But this is the sort of stuff that most well-adjusted people cannot even consider. As I read the words on the computer screen, it chilled me to realize that the disgusting horrors that sick adults inflict on kids not only had to be addressed—these acts had so many twisted variations to them that they each had to be quantified, defined, and reduced to technical terms out of a legal necessity to categorize which degree of a certain crime had been committed. *What a beautiful world*, I thought, wincing as I read each of the bulleted points on the website. "Aggravated sexual battery" was penetration with a finger or object without consent. "Aggravated child molestation" was child molestation that injures the child or involves sodomy—"sodomy" being considered to be unnatural sex acts, which include anal sex and oral sex. Without sounding callous or crude in layman's terms, kindergarten teacher Tonya Craft had been charged with allegedly performing sexual acts with children, putting her fingers or some object inside children's vaginas, and committing some sort of further, even more unnatural sexual act, such as anal sex, through which child victims were injured--twenty-two acts of horrific, life-shattering sexual acts visited upon innocent little girls by my client. This—*if* it had actually occurred—was a major crime!

I turned off the computer, grateful that I had no more lurid details to review, but I couldn't erase the horrible impact of this from my mind. I opened my notes from the meeting with Tonya and studied them, looking for any indication one way or another. I thought of the woman I had met in the law office—bubbly, perky, forthcoming, the last person you could imagine doing anything unpleasant to a child, let alone any of the gut-churning crimes she was charged with. But how could I tell that for sure? Her demeanor was such that I wanted to believe her innocence—but I knew better than to trust a superficial impression. Some people have a special ability to hide the dark sides of their psyches. Tonya Craft might have been exactly as she seemed, a caring, compassionate teacher who treasured and protected the children in her charge. But there was also the possibility to consider—that she was the most cunningly deceptive sociopath I had ever encountered.

I had to know as much as I could. Luckily, when it came to investigations, I had a whole deck of aces up my sleeve.

Part of what made me take this case was the exemplary staff I have working at The LPS Group, Inc. Yes, we are good private investigators—but one of the main associates on my office staff is the best. I knew this remarkable lady would be a key contributor to the overall success of this case, as she has been in many cases in the past. This longtime associate has a strong background in law— a former trial paralegal with over twenty-five years of experience who has killer skills in interpreting both labor and employment law, not to mention knowing her way around civil suits, legal research, and everything in between. She has worked with major, big-guns law firms out of Los Angeles, San Diego, and Atlanta, just to name a few. Her solidly impressive track record made it an easy decision to take this case with her as my right hand. My confidence in her is strong and enduring—and the fact that this paralegal is my wife, Patricia Echols, vice president and chief operations officer of The LPS Group, is beside the point. Patricia has made herself the linchpin of our organization with her hard work and serious dedication, and I could stride fearlessly into battle knowing that this able woman had my back. And, considering the indelicate, emotionally charged facts of this case, I had a sneaking feeling that having a lady involved was going to be an invaluable point.

During a radio interview, I was asked about what my gut feeling was when taking the Tonya Craft case. That question hadn't been previously posed to me before, and I had never given it any thought until I was asked. The Tonya Craft case has provoked an answer if I'm ever asked that question again. So let me preface my answer before I give it.

Let's put the facts on the table. The county where the alleged charges took place is predominantly Caucasian. Ringgold, a very small city, is in Catoosa County, Georgia, a small county next to the Tennessee state line. I'm African-American, I'm from Detroit, Michigan, and I live in Marietta, near Atlanta, the metropolitan capital of Georgia. That makes me an outsider on two counts: on the subject of race, and the ages-old conflict between rural vs. urban populations.

As a professional private investigator, my main purpose is to help those in need. The day I start NOT taking cases because they might be unpleasant, precarious, or even hazardous; or involve people who hold powerful positions or are influential, that is the day I will stop being a private investigator. I call it my creed. This is not something I learned as a private investigator; this is something that was instilled in me as a United States Marine. To "kick ass and take names" means you fight until the fighting is done and take away their spirit, in essence the names, of those you fight.

So, with all of that in mind, here is my answer: My gut told me to be a United States Marine, which has always been my practice.

Good private investigators are a rare breed. At one point in time we were called sleuths. If you have ever seen movies featuring PIs, they are more often than not portrayed as drunken, washed-up ex-cops. Let me tell you, times have changed. I know there are stories out there about unprofessional and unethical behavior displayed by private investigators, but wait a minute— there are also stories about unprofessional and unethical behavior displayed by district attorneys, judges, politicians, police officers, coaches, athletes, men of the cloth, and so on. A very long time ago, I adopted what I call my "Ten Percent Rule": in any single collection of human beings, from every profession or walk of life, there will be 10 percent of them who willfully choose to live on the other side of society's line. The spectrum ranges from those who do things they should not do or display unprofessional or unethical behavior—to those who are out-and-out criminals. In the Tonya Craft case, I saw my Ten Percent Rule in full effect—but I had no idea just how abundantly my theory would be proved.

Moviemakers like to portray the private investigator as being a maverick, a law unto himself; however, this is far from the reality of the business. We have rules, legal constraints, and protocols which we must follow. As a licensed instructor with the Georgia Board of Private Detectives and Security Agencies, it's my duty to ensure that new up-and-coming private investigators know the investigative methods. It's for the benefit of the whole investigative industry that the newbie's are instructed about the fine points of anything which, if not done properly, could be detrimental not only to their careers but also give the whole private investigation industry a black eye. As professional private investigators, our job is to conduct interviews with anyone willing to talk to us in order to gather facts, leads, collect information or validate accounts of incidents. We follow up on leads until they die out, and we investigate anyone and everyone who may be a party to the case we are assigned. While doing this, we conduct overt and covert surveillances, skip traces, background checks, and so on—which entails an enormous amount of research. When working for companies, we also conduct integrity shops and sometimes, depending on the case, executive or personal protection.

The cases we take and the role we play in the process of law is paramount to the flow within the justice system as a whole. The professional PI's role in all cases is to find evidence, if it exists— not to create it. If that evidence cannot be found, then we have to present that along with all of the information located in the course of the investigation and turn it over to the client. In criminal cases, our client is most likely to be the defense attorney. While we're amassing evidence on behalf of the attorney's client, the lawyer is the one who calls the shots as to how that information is to be used. It's up to the defense attorney to know when and how to use the evidence or information in preparation for trial, mediations, or depositions. If, on the other hand, the defense attorney identifies that the evidence or information found is damaging to the defense case or the client, the information now helps prepare the criminal attorney. In that event, the defense must use the damning evidence as a guide to prepare how to defend against it, on the likely assumption that is the evidence will be used by the prosecution. This was the role I played in the Tonya Craft case: For better or worse, it was my job to find the facts.

So where do you begin? What do you start with in a case as big as this one? The usual procedure in my line of work is that it is the client who gives you the directions and tells you what he or she wants. In this case, technically, my clients were Scott and Cary, the attorneys of Slater & King, as they were the ones who hired me. Tonya's attorney in Tennessee, Clancy Covert, was also considered a client. But Tonya Craft herself gave just as much direction—and could you blame her? She was eyeballs-deep in this whole mess. Her life, her entire future, *everything* that Tonya Craft held dear was pivoting on this one point—of proving her innocence. Of course she had a stake in it. It was Psychology 101 that Tonya's insistent involvement in her case came from the knot of fear in her gut, the terrifying feeling that she was trapped in a desperate situation that was spinning madly out of her control, and by God, this determined woman wasn't about to go under without making a brave effort of self-preservation.

She kept her attorneys informed every step along the way, but much of the direction in the case came from her—at least at first. Eventually, Tonya realized that she and I were on the same team. Her confidence in me grew to the point where she told me, "You do what you feel you need to do. I trust you and your judgment."

Once a private investigator has been briefed on the case and accepts an assignment, the investigation begins. In the Tonya Craft case, the assignment was simple: "Conduct background checks, research, surveillance, and interviews, and investigate matters involving *The State of Georgia vs. Tonya H. Craft.*" As long as I complied with the Georgia Laws that govern private investigators and followed the rules set forth by the Georgia Board of Private Detectives and Security Agencies, this assignment was an open invitation to conduct as I saw fit the investigation of the alleged crimes involving Tonya.

This meant I could conduct surveillance, locate witnesses, and interview anyone who would talk or had information to provide about any parties involved in the case, including Tonya. She was, fittingly, the first person in this case that we—the private investigators working for The LPS Group Inc.—investigated. We do this in all our cases, as the client is key to the case, especially a criminal case. There are questions that need to be answered, information to follow up on, and leads that need to be validated. In an investigation in which the client is accused of twenty-two counts of child molestation, a professional private investigator had better investigate that client thoroughly and back again. We never just take the client's word regarding what happened or what they believed happened in a case. We validate the basic underlying truth of the client's story, as it is vital to the outcome and success of the case. But the unusual nature of the Tonya Craft case didn't mean that we didn't have to toe the same lines; many of the research and investigative measures we undertook in this case were routine. However, the stakes were anything but routine, to say the least.

Tonya and I stayed in constant contact.  Throughout the investigation there were times we spoke every day for weeks, even months about the fact of the case, things like what witness I found, what interviews I conducted, what was I working on, this was a consistent occurrence. There were times we talked early in the morning and late at night. I must say this because if you are a private investigator that is married, you know that sometimes you must sit down with your spouse and have "the talk." Married people know exactly what I mean. The last thing an investigation needs on a big criminal case is to have the spouse not being supportive. Thank God I have a strong marriage, and my working this case did not bother Patricia. She did not say anything about it—at least in the beginning.

We began by doing our homework. We initiated an investigation into all the key players involved in the case, which included the parents of the alleged victims: the Lambs, the McDonalds, and the Henkes (Tonya's ex-husband and his new wife). We also had to check out the other players , like the judge, prosecutor, and detectives: Judge Van Pelt, Judge House, Chief District Attorney Chris Arnt, Detective Deal (lead detective on the case), and Detective Stephen Keith. We also investigated the Wilsons, a family with far-reaching connections in the county. Mr. Wilson, the angry father who had threatened Tonya for not passing his daughter, also held a county government office as coroner for Walker County.

Doing our homework provided us with information about the individuals. It gave us their histories, if they had ever been arrested, where they lived and worked, and their occupations. I even used the Open Records Act (ORA) to find out more information about Chris Arnt, Detective Deal, and Detective Keith. The Open Records Act is a wonderful thing. The ORA allows any citizen the right to review confidential documents of any state, city, or county government office and their employees. While personal data maybe redacted out of the personnel files, any pay records, disciplinary actions, reprimands, promotions, training records, and the like is made available to the public. Using the ORA, I was able to pull Arnt's, Deal's, and Keith's personnel files and pore through their records to see if they had received any reprimands, disciplinary actions, or warnings during their employment histories. We looked into Arnt's political campaign for judge to see where his donations came from and how he spent his campaign money. The whole basis of running backgrounds, what I call doing your homework, is to determine what types of people you are dealing with and to find good leads to go follow up. And this particular run of background checks gave me beau coups of material to work with.

My investigation certainly was not initiated or conducted to slander or defame anyone's name or character. However, the story that Tonya explained on the first day we met suggested the type of conspiracy theory that rivaled anything you would see in a movie or read in a suspenseful novel. Tonya's story played over and over in my head throughout the investigation. However, even though she was my client, I couldn't just blindly accept on faith her description of events as being the complete and total truth. As I've mentioned, subjective reality is a slippery thing—and as it goes for any good private investigator, I could not let one subject's version of events dictate how my investigation was conducted. I wasn't hired to be Tonya Craft's fan club; my overriding duty was to the truth. In service to my client I buckled down to conduct this case as impartially and thoroughly as humanly possible. At first glance, this case was looking to become an unholy mess—and I surely wasn't going to add to it by scribbling outside the lines.

## KEY PLAYERS INVESTIGATION

Prior to Tonya's arrest, the Lambs, Wilsons, McDonalds, and Henkes had been all connected with each other in some form or fashion. Some of the connection was due to the children, because they all went to Chickamauga Elementary, were friends with each other, and had sleepovers; some was due to the families having social events together; some was due to a few of the sons playing baseball together on a team where Jerry McDonald was the coach. The families took their vacations together, including a cruise and a trip to Cambodia. All three alleged victims were participants in Tonya's wedding to David Craft, which by the way was held in the home of the Lambs. Sandra had even been the one who had introduced Tonya to David. To stretch this strained chain of connection even further, at one time Tonya had been the Sunday school teacher of Sarah Bass (now Sarah Henke, Joal Henke's current wife). They all knew each other—the lives of these families twisted and intertwined like the strands of a rope. This was a tight group, and Sandra Lamb was its self-declared leader.

## SANDRA LAMB

As I said before, I try to keep an open mind during an investigation. A description of somebody filtered through someone else's words might seem so real when the client relates his or her account of a case for the investigator, but that doesn't mean it's the gospel truth. A story usually has grains of reality in it, to be sure—but it's only a version of reality, and an entirely subjective one. An event which impacts a hundred people can be experienced in a hundred different ways, as those hundred witnesses each filter their testimonies through their own emotions and interpretations. It's a daunting task sometimes, trying to narrow the abstract down to the concrete—but however whipped up, righteously angry, or justified the client might feel, it's only the hard and fast provable facts that make the case, not the emotions it stirs up. Shades of meaning can hide important details and lead the investigator to a wrong conclusion; that's why I like to get it all down and then distill it into strict black and white, all nice and logical like a map. Then I can get an idea of which directions could guide me to the most promising leads.

But to map it out, I needed facts, and I had only been exposed to one side of the story. But I needed more of the story to tie the evidence together.

Tonya's story had not presented Sandra Lamb in a very favorable light, which was no surprise—they were former best friends who'd had a falling-out, so sure, Tonya wouldn't have been showering Sandra with compliments. But the moment Sandra Lamb physically crossed my path, her seemingly crazy and hostile behavior that I personally experienced painted an especially unattractive portrait of the allegedly wronged mother in the case.

I began by observing her routine, day-to-day movements. During the time I conducted surveillance, Sandra Lamb didn't have much of a work routine. Her actions demonstrated a seemingly erratic lifestyle. At various times during the week, the surveillance indicated that Sandra went to work only when she wanted—if she went to work at all. Sandra ostensibly was employed by one of her father's businesses, Duplicator Supply Company, Inc., in Chattanooga, Tennessee, which does about $10 million in annual sales. Her father, French H. Newton, is the owner; Sandra's husband Greg Lamb is vice president of sales. [*Note that at the writing of this book, Greg Lamb and Sandra Lamb are going through a divorce.*] Sandra's father also owned Newton Enterprises, a small firm specializing in antique cars and parts, which did just under $500K per year. It was also alleged that Sandra was on the employment rolls there, too. Whatever her work situation really was, the main fact is that in the small pond of Catoosa County, the members of the Newton family were considered by themselves and certain others to be big fish. While this sort of situation is a standard cliché in Southern potboilers like *Tobacco Road* and *All the King's Men*, its social effect is an undeniable fact of small-town life: big family money in a very little city can make any group of people believe that their higher status actually means that they are powerful, influential, and impervious to consequences for their actions. As identified in the investigation, this generalization fit Sandra Lamb like a well-worn old shoe.

The following incident was telling. In a complex case such as this one, behavior can play a very important role in forming the case theory. As you remember, the first meeting I had with Tonya and the attorneys occurred on July 30, 2008. Almost a year later, on July 24, 2009, I was pulling up to a stop in front of the Lamb house. I had been sent to effect a court-ordered process service to Sandra and Greg Lamb at the Lambs' residence. This order, "Subpoena for the Production of Evidence at a Deposition," was written on July 23, 2009, and was signed by the Superior Court of Catoosa County Clerk Debbie Crowe and witnessed by Judge Ralph Van Pelt Jr. This process was *Civil Action No. 03D2024: Joal Edward Henke, Plaintiff, vs. Tonya Faires Henke (Craft), Defendant*. It requested documents for "any and all cell phone and home phone records showing incoming and outgoing calls from April 1, 2008, to present (July 24, 2009); copies of any cancelled checks to Larry Stagg [Sandra Lamb's attorney] or Chris Arnt [prosecuting district attorney on the Craft case] sent as political contributions for the Superior Court judicial race in 2008 [just in case this information could pertain to the Craft case]; and copies of any and all audiotapes and videotapes where the defendant [Tonya Craft] was discussed.

As a professional private investigator, it is in my best interest to expect the unexpected. Every time a PI conducts a process service, he or she should be prepared for the person to be a difficult service. I always have an audio recorder and/or a video recorder on me to document every word exchanged during the service. I also always make it a point to maintain my sense of professionalism. The calmest situation can erupt into a violent flashpoint, all in a heartbeat and out of nowhere. The way you react is the difference between a professional and a nonprofessional—and I am a pro. Remember my Ten Percent Rule. I wired my audio recorder to pick up every word that was said during the serving of the subpoena.

As I went to effect the process service, Sandra was sitting on her front stoop talking on a cordless phone. At the sound of my approaching vehicle, she looked up and saw me. I knew this because I saw her look up right in my direction and scowl. She well knew the vehicle I drove, a black 2008 Cadillac CTS with rims and tinted windows—it was hard to miss my vehicle in Catoosa County. Some people later asked why I drove this vehicle when serving Sandra Lamb's subpoena. Well, it was a choice of the Cadillac, the motorcycle, or my surveillance vehicle. And since I was actively running a surveillance operation, it would defeat the whole purpose for anyone in Catoosa County to see me in my surveillance vehicle and recognize it. So I drove the Cadillac that day.

I tooled past the Lamb residence, then I did a U-turn and pulled up in front of their house. I parked the Caddy there on the public street with my car facing the exit of the subdivision. As I parked, Sandra got up and trotted quickly into her house, slamming the front door behind her. I walked up the fifty-foot driveway leading to the house and knocked on the door.

My knock was answered—but not by Sandra Lamb. Instead, Sandra's son answered the door. Below is the conversation we had, exactly as transcribed from the audio recording device I was wearing at the time I conducted the process service:

**RECORDED TRANSCRIPT**
**PRIVATE INVESTIGATOR – ERIC ECHOLS**
**AND SANDRA LAMB**

Transcriber's Note: There is a third party who starts the conversation; however, his name is not known. For purposes of this recorded transcript, he shall be referred to as "TP" for third party.

*[Author's Note: "TP" is Sandra Lamb's eighteen-year-old son, Hayden Lamb]*

TP:   Hey man, how you doing'?

EE:   Hey bud, can I see your mom?

TP:   No sir. This is private property. You need to leave.

EE:   I understand, but I need to tell your mom _____. I just got to give her these documents.

TP:   No sir. We're not gonna accept those. This is private property and you need to leave right now.

EE:   Okay. Like I said, I understand that. I just need to give these to your mom. I just saw her on the porch. I need to give 'em to her. I'm just doing my job. I'm just delivering some documents, that's it.

TP:   *[Inaudible]* I'm just doing what I'm told I need to do.

EE:   Okay, but she's here. I just saw her.

TP:   Okay.

EE:   Okay, I'm just trying to give her these documents, man. That's it. It's for her … I ain't trying to…

TP:   Like I said, she knows about this and as I understand we don't have to accept those and…

EE:   There's nothing—okay, it's—so you saying you don't have to accept them. I mean, how old are you?

TP:   Eighteen.

EE:   Okay, so you're eighteen years old. Your mom's here, she just went in the house, I just want to give 'em to her. That's it.

TP:   I've just been told to ask you to leave and that's about all I'm gonna say.

EE:   Okay, so your mom don't want to come and get 'em?

TP:   No.

EE:   That's all I'm trying to do, man.

TP:  I'm just doing what I'm told, brother, I'm sorry.

EE:  I understand.

TP:  Okay.

EE:  But I'm just trying to just give these to you and give them to your mom. Your mom is home. I just saw her run in the house. I hear her right now.

SL:  [*Inaudible*] You know what, you stupid ass son-of-a-bitch.

EE:  Well, you got 'em. You got 'em.

SL:  I didn't sign it and I didn't see it.

EE:  There ain't nothing to sign.

SL:  Get your ass off my property. _____ and I'll call the police right now you stupid ass son-of-a-bitch.

EE:  Ma'am, ma'am.

SL:  _____ your stupid client molested my child and you talk about me and you talk about me to people. I know, people called me about you.

EE:  All right, ma'am. You got 'em. I'm not picking up nothing.

SL:  [Inaudible]

EE:  I'm leaving your property.

SL:  [*Inaudible*]

EE:  Ma'am, I'm leaving your property now.


And I did just that. I turned and started walking back down the walkway in front of the house to the driveway heading to the street. As I reached the walkway, I heard a door slam behind me. I turned and saw all the legal documents I had served heading right toward my head, and here came Sandra Lamb herself, flying at me across her manicured lawn and yelling something unintelligible. I paused long enough to note that she had a cell phone pressed to her ear, no doubt calling the police on me, but nothing in her hands that could be used as a weapon. She was wearing a wrinkled red sundress, her arms and legs pumping as she raced toward my car after me. Her face was a twisted mask of bitter rage.

Betraying no emotion, I opened the Caddy's door and slid into my front seat to wait and see just how her precipitous actions would unfold. The audio device was still recording, but just for backup, I yanked my camera phone off my belt, set it to recording, and held it up in her direction—for a moment feeling more like a vampire slayer brandishing a crucifix at Dracula than a process server delivering documents. I felt glad I had my phone at the ready. Something crazy seemed bound to happen, and whatever was going to go down here, I would be recording it all.

Sandra Lamb came roaring up to my vehicle where I sat parked on the public road, and planted herself right in front of the Cadillac, looking like the very picture of haughty defiance. She stood with one hand on her hip and the other holding the phone to her ear, glaring at me through my windshield and blocking my way out of the subdivision. Her agitated state had brought out the hillbilly twang she no doubt had worked hard to hide. My side window was down, so I had no problem hearing her angry raving clearly—as did the audio and video devices, which captured the whole scene. Below is the official transcript of the bizarre conversation that ensued between us:

> EE: Ma'am, you're in the middle of the road. Ma'am, you're in the middle of the road. Ma'am, you're in the middle of the road.
>
> SL: You know what? The police are coming and I'm glad.
>
> EE Okay, so you're blocking the road now. So you're blocking the road and I can't leave. You're restricting…
>
> SL: Let me tell you something. No, sir, we're not blocking the road…
>
> EE: Ma'am, don't touch me.
>
> [This was her first attempt reach in through my open car window to hit me.]
>
> SL: …so you can't leave.
>
> EE: Don't touch me.

SL: Don't come to my house where my child is that your client molested.

EE: Don't touch me, ma'am.

SL: You can video me all you want to. I'm not gonna touch you.

EE: Okay.

SL: But if you had a little girl that somebody molested –

*[This is where Sandra made an unsuccessful grab for my camera phone, drew back her hand, and then reached back through my car window again and slapped me in the face.]*

SL:   – why don't you shove it up your ass, black bastard.

**[End of transcript.]**

At that point, since she was reaching in through my driver's side window and wasn't in front of my car, I was able to drive out of the subdivision and away from that insanity. I checked my camera phone to make sure that I had caught the whole thing, noting with satisfaction that the phone had worked fine. I then immediately e-mailed the video clip to my office, just in case I was stopped by Catoosa County Sheriff before I left the area. I was protecting the evidence and covering my ass. Let's just say, if I was stopped by Catoosa County Sheriff, I did not want evidence to mistakenly come up missing.

Reality, recorded. I was one happy P.I., all right. I had the main witness against Tonya Craft summed up on tape, and what it revealed was far from positive for Sandra Lamb. As you can tell yourself from the transcription, without a doubt, there is a dark side of Sandra Lamb's personality which can make her become abusive and violent. Even in the face of an investigation in which she was posing as one of the allegedly pained parties, she had no compunctions about being seen as a violent racist. When I later filed an assault charge against Sandra, my recorded evidence of her offensive language, the physical assault, and the racial slur was proof enough.

After the weird street scene with Sandra Lamb, I thought it best to call the Catoosa County Sheriff to report the incident. Based on my investigation and assessment of Sandra, as well as knowing that Sandra was "good friends" with District Attorney Chris Arnt and with Detectives Deal and Keith, my instincts told me Sandra was going to file a report, so I had best file a report, too. But my better judgment told me I'd be a fool to stick around and take care of business there, because I was starting to see considerations outside of the case which gave me pause. At that time, my investigation was focused on the alleged victims' families. I little dreamed that soon, thanks to the Tonya Craft case, I would also be investigating officers within the Catoosa County Sheriff's Department. But just after the disturbing incident with Sandra Lamb, I only had an inkling, an uneasy feeling in my gut that I was entering a country-fried wilderness of mirrors, and that I had better seriously watch and protect myself.

If there really were a network of influence and intrigue operating in Catoosa County, I couldn't expect the same standards of law enforcement I was accustomed to in Atlanta or Marietta. So once I was safely out of Catoosa County heading south on I-75, I made the call to the Catoosa County sheriff's office from my car. Below is the conversation I had with a sheriff's deputy with Catoosa County:

**RECORDED TRANSCRIPT**
**PRIVATE INVESTIGATOR ERIC ECHOLS**
**AND CATOOSA COUNTY SHERIFF'S DEPARTMENT**

CS: How may I help you?

EE: Yes - is this the Catoosa County Sheriff?

CS: Um hum.

EE: Hey, sir, how you doin'?

CS: Fine.

EE: Good. My name is Eric Echols. I'm a private investigator.

CS: Um hum.

EE: And I just did a process serve at a location in Ringgold on Classic Trail. The address is _____ Classic Trail.

CS: Um hum.

EE: Um, the person's name who I served the documents to is Sandra Lamb.

CS: Um hum.

EE: Okay. And the reason why I'm calling is because before I left her property she took a swing at me and hit me; therefore, she assaulted me.

CS: Um hum.

EE: Now, the reason why I'm leaving Catoosa County and not coming down there right this minute is because I know that she's connected with certain people in Catoosa County and I thought it was safe for me just to get on the road and call it in once I got safe on I-75 heading back to Atlanta.

CS: All right.

EE: So I want to make a report.

CS: So you do want to make a report?

EE: Yes, I want to make a report. I got it all on videotape.

CS: You'd have to come back in to Catoosa County.

EE: Okay, well, I'm not coming in with the videotape and all that without me having an attorney with me. But I wanted to make an incident - I can make a phone incident report.

CS: We do not take any incidents over the phone.

EE: Okay, so you can't log this in. You can't?

CS: I can log it in. I can make a note of it. I can let, you know, the lieutenant know, or whoever know. We can't make a report though.

EE: Okay. Well, that's what I want. I want to do that over the phone and then when I come in, then that way I'll have copies of the videotape. I don't want– you have to understand – I'm working a high-profile case in your area and the last thing I want to do is come down there with the videotape and something happens to it.

So I want to go back to Atlanta, make a copy of it and then I'll come in and lodge a formal complaint of assault and battery.

CS: All right, sir. I'll make a note of it and when you feel like when you can come back and talk to someone, just give us a call.

EE: Okay, but you don't have my name. You don't have any of my information.

CS: Hold on. All right, what's your name, sir?

EE: My name is Eric Echols.

CS: All right. A phone number I can reach you at?

EE: What is that that you need?

CS: A phone number I can reach you at?

EE: My phone number is 770-579-0188.

CS: All right, so I got your name, your phone number. What's your address?

EE: 1050 East Piedmont Road. I'm in Suite E, as in Eric, 134, that's Marietta, Georgia, 30062.

CS: Um hum.

EE: And what's your name, Officer?

CS: My badge number is 921.

EE: Your badge number is 921.

CS: Um hum.

EE: Okay, I don't get a name?

CS: No, sir.

EE: Okay, just your badge number is 921?

CS: Um hum. Um hum.

EE: Okay. Is there anything else you need?

CS: No, sir.

EE: Okay.

CS: Just call us - call this number back and tell us where you want to meet and when you want to meet.

EE: Okay, sounds good.

CS: All right.

EE: Thank you very much.

CS: Yup.

*[End of transcription.]*

There it is, word for word on the complete, start-to-finish transcript of the conversation. Even allowing for the fact that Ringgold, Georgia, is a tiny town, this was an appallingly unacceptable and unprofessional response to a citizen by a member of law enforcement. It makes no difference where that is. When you wear the badge, there are ironclad rules and responsibilities that go with it whether the beat is city sidewalks or country roads, the badge—after all is a display of honor, pride, professionalism, it's a symbol of right, we're not in the day of Deputy Barney Fife anymore. But after I hung up my cell phone in frustration, I couldn't help but think that Barney would have done a better job of taking my report.

Whoever he really was, it's readily apparent that Badge Number 921 was lackadaisical and indifferent to the point of not even bothering to ask me my name or any details of my complaint. You can see it there in print, how a sizable chunk of his side of the conversation was no more than noncommittal grunts, non-responses that indicated to me a callous, insensitive attitude. Or had he already been notified by Sandra of the incident that occurred at her home and had no intention of taking a report from me? All reports pertaining to the incident in question should have been made a part of the record—that is what police departments do, just as I do as a licensed private investigator. We take reports in case it turns out that they matter in an investigation—but Badge Number 912 must have been out sick the day professional ethics were taught at the Police Academy.

Back at LPS headquarters, I checked the records, where I was able to find out one thing that was for certain: Sandra did file a police report on 07/24/09, Case Number 090700613. The reporting officer was Steve Crossen, Badge Number 573. Below is the incident report the officer took, based on the testimony of Sandra Lamb:

CATOOSA COUNTY S. O.                    **INCIDENT REPORT**                  CASE NUMBER

GA0230000                                                                     090700613

                                                                              Page 2

NARRATIVE                    Reporting Officer:   573        STEVE CROSSEN

THE COMPLAINANT ADVISED A BLACK MALE DRIVING A CADILLAC CAME TO HER RESIDENCE TO SERVE HER CIVIL PAPERS IN REFERENCE TO AN ONGOING CASE INVOLVING HER CHILD. SHE ADVISED WHEN THE SUBJECT PULLED INTO HER DRIVEWAY SHE WENT INTO THE RESIDENCE TO AVOID SERVICE AS ADVISED BY CHRIS ARNT, AN ATTORNEY, FRIEND OF HERS.
THE COMPLAINANT ADVISED ONCE SHE WAS INSIDE THE RESIDENCE, THE BLACK MALE KNOCKED ON THE DOOR. HER SON ANSWERED THE DOOR AND THE MALE WAS SAYING "WHERE IS SHE, I KNOW SHE'S HERE." THE COMPLAINANT ADVISED HER SON TRIED TO SHUT THE DOOR AND THE BLACK MALE SUBJECT PUT HIS HAND ON THE DOOR AND WOULDN'T ALLOW THE DOOR TO SHUT.
SHE ADVISED WHILE THE DOOR WAS OPEN THE BLACK MALE SUBJECT THREW THE PAPERS INSIDE THE RESIDENCE. SHE ADVISED THE SUBJECT WOULD NOT PROVIDE THEM WITH IDENTIFICATION. AN EXTRA PATROL WAS PLACED ON THE RESIDENCE IN REFERENCE TO THIS MALE SUBJECT.

MLT

When reading the narrative of the reporting officer provided by Sandra, note these following quoted statements:

1. "...to serve her civil papers in reference to an ongoing case involving her child."
2. "The subject pulled into her driveway."
3. "...she went into the residence to avoid service as advised by Chris Arnt, an attorney friend of hers."
4. "The male was saying, 'Where is she, I know she's here.'"
5. "The complainant advised her son tried to shut the door and the black male subject put his hand on the door and wouldn't allow the door to shut."
6. "She advised the subject would not provide them with identification."

7. "An extra patrol was placed on the residence in reference to this male subject."

As a private investigator, I am well aware that all documents, reports, recordings, and anything relating to your case must be investigated to ascertain fact. What made the police incident report from Sandra disputable was that I had the hard facts and the solid taped evidence that showed an entirely different version of the events as alleged by Sandra Lamb. While Sandra certainly knew that I had videotaped her at my vehicle, what she did not know was that I had had a recording device on throughout the entire incident. Everything was audio taped from the point when I first knocked on the door of the Lamb residence.

Let me break down the seven noted statements:

1. The papers that were being served had nothing to do with her daughter. In fact, the process service was for producing specific evidence in the case of *Joal Henke v. Tonya Craft*.

2. I never pulled into the Lambs' driveway. The video evidence showed that I was parked on the street and that Sandra stood in the street in front of my vehicle. On the audiotape, you can hear me walking out to the street to my vehicle.

3. Chris Arnt is not just an attorney or an assistant district attorney; he is the chief district attorney for Catoosa County and the prosecuting attorney in the Tonya Craft case. Sandra identified Chief District Attorney Chris Arnt as a friend of hers and said that her friend Chris Arnt told her not to accept a court-ordered subpoena, an official court document which had been signed by the Georgia superior court judge of Catoosa County.

4. Reading the transcript, you can see that I never once stated the phrase alleged in Sandra Lamb's report: "Where is she, I know she is here."

5. From the transcript of the audiotape, there was no sound of a struggle with the Lamb's front door, nor was there any comment from Sandra or her son indicating that I had my hand on the door or that I would not allow the door to shut.

6. A person effecting a process service is not required to show ID. If either of the Lambs had asked me for it, I would have presented a business card—but as you can plainly read in the transcript, Sandra already knew who I was and why I was there.

7. I cannot confirm or deny whether an extra patrol by the Catoosa County Sheriff was provided for the Lamb residence. I would like to see the duty log for that shift. But you tell me—who do *you* know who can get police coverage for their home based on something as flimsy as this? Hey, I'm only asking a question.

The audio and video recordings clearly repudiated the version of the incident as sworn to by Sandra in her police report. The discrepancy between the actual recorded events and her description of the incident cast doubt on not only on the integrity and character of Sandra Lamb, but also her many statements in this case. These were more like the actions of a deceitful person who was willing to do what it takes to control a situation—including having anyone arrested who was on the opposite side of a legal case she was involved in, even someone who was at the time acting in the service of the court as a process server. The camera phone video I made at the time clearly shows that Sandra

Lamb—almost immediately after she stated she wasn't going to touch me—then physically assaulted me with a sharp slap in the face and called me, quote-unquote, a "black bastard." Based on the evidence found in the investigation, could it be assumed that this blithe willingness to play fast and loose with reality betrayed a manipulative side of Sandra Lamb? I tried to get into that mind of hers, such as it was, to figure out what her game could be and how it related to the case. Her true motivations seemed baffling—but within this apparent explosion of emotion were nuggets of cold, hard fact.

As crazy as her behavior seemed, Sandra Lamb knew conclusively that her tirade in the middle of the street was all on the record. She saw me holding up my camera phone she even made a grab for it to take it away from me, all of it caught on tape as she glared right into the lens. When she failed to snatch my camera phone, she went all "sweet lemons" about it, stating, "You can video me all you want to," so it's not like she could maintain her ignorance of being recorded. But in light of the incident being openly videotaped for evidence and Sandra's own admission on the record that she understood that her every word and move was being officially documented, her behavior was totally off the chain.

Whether she had wanted to or not, this street scene of hers gave me a wealth of subtext about the character of Sandra Lamb. Her over-the-top reaction gave me the distinct impression that this was a person who considered herself to be above the law— this strident, red-faced, shouting woman thought she was an exception to the rules that govern everyone else. I had noted how she loudly made it a point to identify Chief District Attorney Chris Arnt as a close personal friend, which was apparently the reason she thought she had carte blanche to do what she wanted to do to whomever she wanted to do it, with no worries or fears about law enforcement. In fact, it seemed that she already had a comfortable arrangement with the local police—or perhaps it was simply that her family name carried enough weight in the county to get special consideration. It was stated on the police report that due to the incident with me, Sandra would receive an extra police patrol at her residence. Put *yourself* into this equation, and think: If *you* had physically assaulted a person in his face, spitting out a hostile epithet like "black bastard"—and knowing that the true version of the incident had been captured on tape—would you have enough brass *cojones* to call your local police about it afterward and demand that they patrol your residence? In a well-functioning society, that idea wouldn't go far—but I wasn't in a well-functioning society. I was in Catoosa County, Georgia.

The whole ugly incident and its immediate repercussions only added to my investigative conclusions about Sandra Lamb—and to my increasing sense of foreboding about the whole Tonya Craft case. I drove back to civilization, turning the events over and over in my mind and trying to trace patterns in the still-murky big picture. Sandra Lamb's actions and the police deputy's pointedly bored disinterest were certainly drawing a map for me, but it wasn't one that would give me a reassuring sense of direction. This case was making me wish that I was on the job anywhere else—even Detroit looked like an improvement in comparison. I let out a dark chuckle and shook my head. At least a huge, sprawling, populous city like Detroit was the devil I knew—but up here, in this hill-country smallville...? It was becoming disturbingly clear that my investigation was going to be conducted within a remote backwater realm where the usual rules could be tossed out the window on a whim.

Now I knew precisely what Kevin Costner had meant with that line in the movie *JFK*. I had the feeling that I was definitely through the looking glass on this one.

## JOAL HENKE

Joal Henke was a vital subject of my investigation. One reason was because he was the father of Tonya's daughter, whom as you know was one of the alleged victims. Joel also was one of the prosecution's main witnesses. Besides that major point, there was compelling reason of the complaint about inappropriate contact between Joal's new wife and Tonya's daughter. The unsavory details coming to light in this case made me question everything twice; everyone who had played any kind of a role in all this was under my scrutiny, and no one was to be taken at face value. As I clicked through Joal Henke's file, my mind ran to the basic questions I always asked myself over and over on an investigation: *What is* really *going on here? Who stands to benefit, and how?* And: *Who among the players knows what the underlying game is?* I studied a photograph of the subject and tried to see beneath the smiling mask.

Joal Henke was one of those people who presented themselves well, was a good communicator, and kept up a well groomed image—the type who took a good picture and looked like he knew it. As I examined his photo, my investigator's brain sized him up: Joal Henke, about 5'9 to 5'10, between 175 and180 pounds, a suburban professional go-getter with an athletic build. Tonya had stated in an interview that Joal used his looks and personality to get what he wanted. He reminded me of the young Bruce Willis back when the series *Moonlighting* was playing. Joal worked as a realtor for Keller Williams in Chattanooga, Tennessee. At one point, he was employed as a fitness instructor who also taught classes in karate and taekwondo.

The LPS Group's investigation into Joal would include the same mobile surveillance routine we had done on Sandra Lamb. It was my wild hope to catch Joel and Sandra meeting up together in an extramarital affair. I'm not just throwing that out to add juice or to imply the actual existence of an affair between the two of them— but according to the information I had gleaned during one of the many information-gathering interviews I had with Tonya, there was a repeating pattern at work here. Tonya had stated that when she and Joal were married, he had been caught cheating on her. Tonya had discovered this painful fact through another private investigator she had hired before we ever met, and that PI had caught Joal in an extramarital affair with another woman. During this same conversation, she also stated that Joal had been married once before he married Tonya; his first wife had also caught Joal cheating with another woman, which in turn had led to their divorce.

This information drew a picture of a guy whose wedding ring seemed to give him the itch to wander. I've seen plenty of that type in my previous investigations, and there's a general feeling among almost every single one of them that even while he is sneaking around, he is invisible as well as invulnerable—the perfect combination for making a stupid, careless slip-up that could break a case wide open. If Joal indeed had previously been involved in infidelity with other women, the distinct likelihood of catching Sandra Lamb and Joal meeting up for a hookup was not farfetched. Confirming an intimate relationship between two of the parents of the alleged victims would be a major discovery in the investigation. This discovery could have opened the doors to the existence of some sort of a conspiracy to get Tonya for a personal grudge. I was still a bit dubious, though, to the full acceptance of Tonya's word on the matter. Her own experience with Joal's acts of infidelity could be validated by having Tonya contact that PI that detected the affair and direct them to share their information with me. But as for Tonya knowing about Joal cheating during his first marriage, I would have to confirm that with Joal's first wife.

I located Joal Henke's first wife by following up on the lead provided by Tonya. For the sake of protecting her name and privacy I will call her Wife #1. I located Wife #1 living in Ringgold, Georgia, in Catoosa County. The first time I went to Wife #1's residence, I noted as I pulled up on the street that the address was in a pleasant middle-income neighborhood with a very quiet and tranquil country suburban atmosphere. Wife #1's house was a tidy little home wood-frame, small and neat with a well-manicured lawn, but the driveway was empty. I rang the bell and knocked at the front door, but there was no answer. I tucked one of my business cards for The LPS Group between the glass storm door and the frame with a scrawled notation: "Please call me." I was hoping the professional look of my business card would inspire enough confidence in her to really call me, because I just *love* to talk to people on a case.

I'm not kidding. Sometimes the easy part of my job is talking to people. I just have to figure out who the right ones are and *boom* I'm on my way. Getting people to open up to me is a natural talent I have. When I started doing investigations in retail, I was employed as an investigator by a company who had me conduct in-house theft interviews with employees who were under suspicion of employee theft. I would interview these suspects over the phone—

and I would get almost immediate out-and-out admissions of guilt from them. Really! I would call them up, talk to them a little bit on the phone—and **bingo!** I could get them to admit to thefts they had committed while working for the company. Over the phone! Once I got them started, I'd just sit there quietly listening as the people spilled their guts. I could even get the employee on the other end of the line to write out a statement admitting his or her own stealing in detail and revealing any knowledge of other theft activity that was occurring at the company.

When I became a private investigator and began investigating criminal and civil cases, I took on a different approach, knocking on the door. That worked better for me than cold calls on the phone. Using the phone method, if you want information and you are working a criminal or civil case and you call the person on the phone, it is too easy for that person to just hang up the phone. Either that or the anonymous voice on the other end will just tell you the person you're looking for is out, or doesn't live there anymore.  This typically happens when the caller wants information and the called does not know who it is on the other end.

But if you do it in person, you stand to get better results. It's much more difficult for people to ignore someone knocking on the door and standing on their doorstep; it's even more difficult for people to slam the door in your face if you are standing right there looking them in the eye; and it's really difficult for people to say, "I don't want to talk to you," when you are there in front of them— especially if you are professionally trained to get people to talk. Hanging up was not a problem in the retail investigations, because the employee knew who I was and what department I was in, and I knew that I had the correct phone number. However, in the Tonya

Craft case, I was not a known quantity, though I imagine most of the players had already heard of me through the grapevine. Calling them up out of the blue wouldn't yield the real results I was looking for, So going to the residences or job locations of those I needed to talk to was part of my investigative plan, as I knew if I were there in front of the person I could get them to talk and get the information I needed for the case. This was no different for Wife #1.

On June 20, 2009, I went back to the residence of Wife #1. Initially there was no answer at the door, but this time, I could see there was a vehicle in the driveway and the garage door was open. This was a sign that someone was home, and they're not answering the door was because they were perhaps indisposed or not far away, maybe over at a neighbor's house visiting. So I decided to do a surveillance to observe any movement. I went back to my car and sat.

The minutes stretched out. The tranquility of that neighborhood was like a rocking cradle and I was getting bored. Luckily, I keep a book tucked into the door panel for these types of surveillances where all I was looking for was a sign that someone was home. Right then I was immersed in *The Fisherman and the Catch: Catching the Right Women* by Ric D. Harris. In it, the author humorously describes the different types of women, based on factors like behavior, style, and personality, and then relates them to different types of fish. It was a hilarious read, and was I grateful for it. Judging from Harris's description, Tonya Henke Craft would be a bass to some men. I laughed out loud. Sandra Lamb, I thought, would be more of a catfish or barracuda.

After about an hour or so, I observed a female coming out the garage, going to the vehicle as if to check for something. She was a petite woman who obviously kept herself in shape, with a thin but graceful figure. Her ash-blond hair was shoulder-length with soft waves in it. I immediately got out of my vehicle and made my approach. As I got near, she straightened up and saw me. I expected narrowing eyes, but she smiled at me pleasantly and said, "Hey, there. Can I help you with something?" Her voice had a faint southern sound. I was glad to meet a local who did not look at me like I had three eyes, or treat me as an out-of-area interloper.

I smiled back and asked, "Excuse me, ma'am—are you by any chance [*using the name of Wife#1*]?" She nodded, still pleasant but with an edge of confusion, and confirmed her name. I began to introduce myself. "Good afternoon, my name is Eric. I'm a private investigator investigating a child molestation case in which your ex-husband Joal Henke is involved—"

Her answer was so immediate it startled me. "Oh no," she blurted, her voice almost a moan of dread. The tone of her response carried a message that to me implied that she thought I had shown up on her doorstep investigating Joal Henke for child molestation. I thought fast. The way I had just introduced myself to Wife #1 was in no way misleading, but her interruption made it incomplete. I hadn't had the chance to specify anything, such as for whom I was looking, for whom I was working, what angle I was pursuing, it had all been left open- ended, and Joal's first wife took it and ran with it right to the conclusion that I was after Joal for the crime. This was an unforeseen opportunity, I realized. Wife #1 looked like a bucket full of secrets that was ready to tip over, and I didn't want to say anything that would make her over think things right then. I wanted the unvarnished reaction. So I kept quiet about the rest of it and let Joal's first wife fill in the silent, unsaid spaces.

As a Certified Forensic Interviewer, I'm trained to ask questions and make comments or statements to solicit a response or reply, so that I can read the body behavior, expressions, and replies to see how I should follow up with my next question or statement. My reply to Wife #1 was "I know, I know," to imply that I agreed with her thought. Having done my homework on Wife #1, I knew she also had a daughter from a previous marriage. Having this information, I began talking to her about the relationship between the girl and Joal. Wife #1 stated that Joal was always around kids and that his relationship with her daughter was "like a line drawn in the sand—either she liked him or hated him." Now during all this we were outside and it was hot. I'm a bald brother, so the heat was pounding on my head and I was sweating. I pulled out my handkerchief and began wiping away. Wife #1 looked at me with concern and said, "Let's go into the house, where it is cool."

It sounded good to me. I said, "Please, if we could—I'm melting." She turned and led the way into her home. While her back was to me, I reached into my breast shirt pocket and hit *record* on my recording device. Yes—she was certainly a nice lady, but I'm not stupid. I wanted a record as to what was said the entire time I was in her home.

Once we were inside the house, I was surprised again. She led me to her front room and waved a hand toward the sofa, saying in her pleasant voice, "Please have a seat." I noted the standard country-home furnishings, the dark wood coffee table and the homey pattern on the sofa cover. She disappeared and returned with a glass of ice water for me, then took a seat on the overstuffed chair. As I set the glass down on a coaster, I asked her as delicately as I could if, when she was married to Joal, her daughter ever stated that Joal was inappropriate with her. Again, I was watching for a verbal or behavioral response. The response I was looking for is what we trained interviewers call an "emphatic or definite denial," something along the lines of "Absolutely not!" or "My daughter would have told me if something like that was happening"—but, especially taking into account her initial reaction, the response that I got rang my hard-wired Marine's buzzer.

Wife #1 smiled a small smile and, with a hint of something approaching optimism in her voice, she calmly replied that her daughter had never mentioned anything, and she had never suspected anything. There was no shifting in the way she was sitting, no rise in the tone of her voice, no rising of the eyebrows—her impassive response seemed drained of emotional conviction in my eyes. The way she had phrased it seemed like a deliberate psychological sidestep—saying that her daughter never mentioned anything could have meant something had occurred with Joal but her daughter had simply never *said* anything to her about it, perhaps because the daughter was never asked or did not think the mother would believe her. It could also have meant nothing untoward with Joal ever did happen. Or it could mean that something had happened which Wife #1 knew but was in total denial about, and this verbal distancing was the way she shielded herself from the nasty reality of it.

Her response that she never suspected anything only indicated to me that she never personally saw anything to raise suspicion. And in the forefront of my mind was the fact that Joal had carried on an extramarital affair right under this poor woman's nose, and that she hadn't had a clue about it. There were too many doubts with her response, behavior, and reaction to my question especially considering the way our conversation had begun with her implication that Joal was the target of a child-molestation investigation. As an interviewer, I was looking for something in particular, and this subject did not respond in that manner. It just wasn't adding up.

During our conversation, still reading her body language and analyzing her comments, I gently asked her if she would call her daughter and inquire if Joal displayed any inappropriate behavior with her. Wife #1 stated in a firm but anxious tone that she would call her daughter and ask her if Joal had shown any inappropriate behavior. The way she looked and how she responded is how any mother would respond when a thought suddenly flashes in her mind that someone may have done something unspeakable to her baby. Her demeanor at this point indicated to me a mother who was concerned and wanted to be 100 percent sure that her little girl had not been harmed in any way. Wife #1 added that while her daughter was out about two or three years ago (which would have been 2006 or 2007), her daughter had run into Joal. The two of them had spoken briefly, during which time Joal had impulsively apologized, as the girl had phrased it, for his behavior and trying to be her dad. The remark about "his behavior" is what concerned me. Wife #1 did state that she never heard of Joal being inappropriate with any of the kids he was around when they were married.

I didn't show my disappointment, but Wife #1 was scarcely turning out to be the tidal wave of evidence I had anticipated. But there was something there in her odd reactions, a nugget of truth that I had to translate. For that I needed further leads. As an investigator, at this point my goal was to get names and any contact information of the children Joal was around or had a friendship with, those he trained in karate and taekwondo, and those children who were around Joal's residence at the time he was married to Wife #1. Most importantly and solely based on this interview with Wife #1, I believed that contact with her daughter was warranted. Wife #1 left too many uncertainties and doubts as to whether in fact Joal displayed any inappropriate behavior or contact with her daughter, and only the daughter could confirm or rule out whether Joal had displayed any inappropriate behavior toward her or any other child she knew who was around their residence.

Now let me tell you why this was so important. It was that creepy pube-shaving incident in the shower with Joal's current wife, Sarah Bass Henke, and Tonya's six-year-old daughter that Tonya had reported to family services in Tennessee. Now, if Joal was involved in acts of child molestation or any type of inappropriate behavior with a child during his marriage to Wife #1, and it was further reported that Joal's current wife Sarah was involved in inappropriate behavior with Tonya's six-year-old daughter, this information could be used to add to the defense of Tonya. Or, on the off chance that Tonya would be found not guilty of these crimes, this information could be used to assist her in the event of any custody battle for her children once acquitted. Knowing the comments made by Wife #1 and about the "like-hate relationship" between Wife #1's daughter and Joal, my investigation led me to make contact with the daughter of Wife #1. Remember, as a professional private investigator, my role in any case is to investigate, meaning to gather information and validate the information as being factual or not. Wife #1 could only tell me what she believed the relationship was between her daughter and Joal. She admitted that she didn't know what actually had happened and further stated that only her daughter could provide specific details as to why she did not like Joal and whether or not in fact any inappropriate behavior had taken place. The girl in question was now grown and in her mid-twenties. I asked Wife #1 if she would get in touch with her daughter and provide her my contact information. Wife #1 promised me that she would contact her for me.

On July 22, 2009, I was contacted by Wife #1's daughter by phone. [*To protect the lady's privacy, she will be identified here only as Jane Doe.*] The phone conversation with Jane was very interesting. I introduced myself as a private investigator working on a child molestation case and said that I was investigating Joal Henke. This was a solid introduction; I clearly identified myself. Jane didn't seem very reserved; talking to her mother first seemed to have helped build a little creditability and trust for me, and made sure that I said nothing leading—meaning that I did not state specifically what the mother had told me about her daughter's relationship with Joal. I went on to say that I had spoken with her mom, and based on that conversation, I wanted to talk with Jane, the daughter, to see if there were any issues stemming from her past relationship with Joal Henke that might play into this investigation I was doing now. With an introduction like this, I was expecting for Jane to say, "What in the hell are you talking about?" In a response that mirrored her mother's disarming "oh, no" reply, immediately Jane blurted out, "I hated Joal."

That was all. Three words, spoken in a firm, righteous voice of utter conviction: "I hated Joal."

This is what you call a definite direct response—there was no hesitation or pause as if Jane needed to think of what to say in reply, there was no timid, soft tone as if she were afraid of her past demons. Her reply was unyielding and solid. Remember in the 1984 movie "A Soldier's Story," when Captain Davenport asks Private Wilkie how he feels about Sergeant Waters, and in a tone dripping with conviction, the soldier replies, "I despised him"? That's the feeling I got over the phone when Jane told me, "I hated Joal." When I asked why she hated him, she stated, "He is cocky, arrogant, and full of himself"—pretty much the same as Tonya had described him. Jane then explained to me that the age differences of each of them also played into her inability to get along with Joal. Jane said that Joal was ten years younger than her mother, and ten years older than Jane. Jane was twelve years old when Joal, who was twenty-two, and her mother, thirty-two, were married. On my note pad, I sketched out a triangle and scribbled the three ages down at the points. I was adding the initials of each member of this weird family arrangement when I was caught short in my thoughts by Jane's next remark:

"Joal was a pervert."

Hearing Joal described with the word "pervert" from someone who had had no contact with him in ages led me to believe Jane had stories to tell that she had been holding back for years. I leaned in, holding the receiver closer to my ear. Jane could be the source of that flood of secrets I had sensed would come from her mother, and I didn't want to miss a word. I immediately made sure my phone recorder was on and tightly secured to the receiver.

I could almost hear her blush over the phone as Jane explained how she had developed very early, stating that at the age of eleven she was already wearing a C-cup bra. Being like most men, I didn't know from cup sizes; I truly had no idea if a C-cup for an eleven-year-old was normal or not; but from the fact that Jane had made a point of it told me that this was unusual for that age. It was enough to attract attention, and for a child that age, it was all unwelcome. But the most unwelcome attention came from Joal Henke. Jane told me that Joal, would make embarrassing comments about her breast. Jane remembered that one time she and the family went to an amusement park, and when they were getting on a ride, Joal made a comment to her boyfriend about Jane's breasts. The teens were speechless, with no idea how to respond. Later when the youngsters were alone, the boyfriend asked her what that was all about, saying, "That was freaky, and it creeped me out." I asked Jane what exactly were the comments he had made, and Jane replied how Joal would make it sound like a flattering compliment, saying things about how nice her breasts were. Sometimes he would joke with her uneasy boyfriend about the size of them. Even when he wasn't saying anything about them, she knew he was watching her intently, and it made her shudder.

I asked Jane if there were any times that Joal made any physical advances toward her. Jane said she remembered one weird situation. She paused for a moment to collect her thoughts, and then began to explain.

One evening when she was feeling very sick, she went downstairs to lie on the couch. While she was lying on the couch, Joal came in. He gently nudged the girl over and for a moment, he sat there beside her on the edge of the couch, asking her if she was feeling better. Jane didn't want to talk to him. She felt miserable enough with whatever bug she had picked up, so she just murmured sleepily and turned away from him, hoping he'd take the hint and go away. She felt the pressure on the edge of the couch give as he stood up, but her relief changed to troubled confusion as she realized he was simply changing his position. He squeezed himself flat on the edge of the couch to lie behind her, effectively trapping the girl and preventing her escape. Jane went on to say that Joal then reached over her and put his arm around her waist, pulling her close to him. Jane told me that she did not see why lying behind her was necessary and felt it was a weird and uncomfortable situation—but the girl was too scared and confused to make a sound, so the two of them lay there in the darkening living room for what seemed like forever. Jane stated that she did not recall whether Joal put his hands down her pants or up her shirt during this incident. The troubling thing was that some parts of this memory had faded into fever dream that Jane had never been able to sort out later. She could never remember Joal getting up and leaving the room. She just knew that when she finally awoke, he was gone, and she was alone on the couch.

Jane admitted that she really had nothing more tangible than that, that Joal had mostly only made perverted comments about her. Still, this was bombshell evidence in this sort of case. In the thirty minutes I had to talk with Jane over the phone, it validated some important points—that Joal had made inappropriate comments toward a minor; but I found it somewhat telling that Jane had stated, "I can't recall" if Joal ever put his hands down her pants or up her shirt. This remark indicated to me a possibility that Joal could have put his hands down her pants or up her shirt, but it happened so long ago she could have blocked it out. I make this observation purely based on being a Certified Forensic Interviewer. *If* in fact Joal did *not* touch Jane inappropriately, she would have stated with 100 percent certainty, "He never did that," or "That never happened," or "He did not." That "I can't recall" implies he could have, and she just doesn't remember or she was not going to tell me over the phone due to not knowing me or she could have been embarrassed. There are many reasons Jane could not have remembered or did not want to talk about it. I'm not the one to say whether or not Joal did touch Jane in a sexually inappropriate manner; however, I will say that Jane speaking to someone in the field of psychology might unlock some information.

Jane also remembered a situation that involved a childhood friend of hers. I will leave his name out to protect his privacy as well and will refer to him as James Doe. Unlike Wife #1 and her daughter, James Doe wrote me a statement (which you will read in a moment). Jane told me that James at the time was a neighbor who lived around the block from her house and would hang out at their home, sometimes running errands for Joal. Jane said that James came to her, claiming that he had caught Joal dead to rights running around on her mother [*Wife #1*]. Jane wanted to tell her mother, but she stated that James told her that Joal said he would kill him if his wife found out. Jane told James that was ridiculous, that Joal would not kill him—but she stated that James remained so terrified that she never told her mother what he had told her about Joal's double life. Two months later, however, James was proved right when Joal's chickens came home to roost. This time, Jane's mother caught Joal cheating with the same lady James had seen Joal with.

My findings disturbed me. This case was getting uglier with every step. I was torn: on the one hand, I was sadden by under covering and opening old wounds of possible child abuse and molestation; on the other hand, given the nature of the crimes, the fact that I was on the right track about Joal it almost made me feel relieved. With what I was uncovering, I had some direct confirmation of past inappropriate behavior that had been demonstrated by Joal Henke. But even though Jane seemed honest and forthcoming when she explained to me the incidents she remembered, I had to have corroboration. As an investigator, a rule of thumb is to have two people validate or confirm what an interviewee says. Knowing this and practicing this rule, I needed to track down James Doe.

Following up on the leads provided by Jane, on June 30, 2009, I located James Doe in South Georgia. He was currently an inside guest of the federal government at Valdosta State Prison, where he was incarcerated on a drug conviction charge. I contacted Valdosta State Prison to arrange a visitation with James. Since I was not a family member, I had to get special permission for my visitation, and to get that special permission, I had to inform Valdosta State Prison why I needed to talk to James Doe. When I explained my reason, I was informed they required a letter faxed to the warden's office from Tonya Craft's attorneys on their letterhead stating the reasons I needed to talk to James Doe. I immediately contacted Scott and Cary King to request a letter be sent to Valdosta State Prison on my behalf. On the letterhead of Slater & King, dated July 3, 2009, the following official letter of request was sent:

Re: Request for Interview with Inmate
Inmate: James Doe [Legal name of inmate changed for privacy.]
Our Investigator; Eric D. Echols, The LPS Group, Inc.
Investigator License #'s PDSG043727 & CFTR000992

Dear Warden Danforth,

The undersigned and this law firm represent Tonya Henke Craft in a case styled the State of Georgia vs. Tonya Craft, 2008 SU-CR-534 which is currently awaiting trial in Catoosa County, Georgia.

In that regard and to assist in the defense of Mrs. Craft, this firm has employed Eric Echols and The LPS Group, Inc., to assist in various aspects of trail preparation, to include without limitation, interviewing key witnesses. We have recently become aware of information known to [*Legal name of inmate*], an inmate at Valdosta State Prison/Lowndes Unit, which we believe will assist us in our defense of Mrs. Craft and therefore request you allow Mr. Echols to interview [*Legal name of inmate*] at the prison as soon as possible. Mr. Echols has already spoken with Ms. Gail Knowles in your office and I believe this letter is all that you need to grant our request. However, if more is required, please advise so that we can comply immediately.

As her trail could possibly be as early as September 2009, time is of the essence of our request and we would greatly appreciate your prompt attention. Thank you in advance for your assistance in this matter.

Sincerely yours,
[Signature of Cary King]
Cary S. King
Attorneys    for    Tonya

Craft

On July 6, 2009, I was notified by Valdosta State Prison that approval was granted for me to meet and interview James Doe. The interview was set for July 13, 2009, at 1:00p.m. I must admit, this was the first time I ever had interviewed someone in prison. As a matter of fact, this was the first time I'd ever been to a prison or even a jail. My work had sometimes resulted in putting a criminal behind bars, but I only had gone through the process as far as the courtroom. Now it was time to see the other end of the justice equation. This would be a totally new experience for me, and I was more than up for the challenge.

But when I arrived at Valdosta State Prison, my Marine's bravado suddenly waned. A broad, flat expanse had been hacked out of the Georgia pine forest, and in the center of this desolation laid the sprawling prison complex. The sight of the place alone was enough to make me tighten up. Everything looked even more ominous shimmering in the South Georgia summer heat. The perimeter was an electrified fence punctuated with tall guard towers and topped with wicked-looking razor wire, which highlighted the sharp edges when hit by the sunlight. In the distance, the long, low dormitory buildings stood in rows, looking like something between a chicken farm and a concentration camp. I could not imagine what it would be like to live inside that place, or even be locked up for a short time. Little did I dream what Catoosa County had in store for me—but I'm getting ahead of myself. Right now, Valdosta State Prison looked to be as much human hell as I thought I could endure.

As I was screened and allowed to walk through the prison gates, I felt as though I had done something wrong. Just the pure sight of a prison can make a person feel like he or she had better not ever break the law. At that moment, I was damned glad to have been living a clean life and keeping up with the ethical requirements of my profession. Still, I clenched.

Once I got inside the prison. I was taken to a secured area where I could talk with James Doe. As we walked along the echoing corridor, one of the officers asked me if I were an attorney. I chuckled, and answered, "No, I'm a private investigator following a lead."

The correction officer said, "It really must be a good lead."

"I hope so," I replied. The officer escorted me to the door of a small holding room and told me to wait there for my conference with James Doe. Some thirty long minutes later, I was still sitting alone in this hot room on a metal stool. I wondered if I had been stuck there in that room so long that I had been forgotten—perhaps I had become an inmate. But there was no chance I could be forgotten, because I was on display like a hamster in a pet store. The small room was surrounded by glass, and all the officers from the control room were looking at me. It reminded me of the old HBO series *Oz,* when all the inmates would be in their pods and the officers could watch their every move.

Finally, on the other side of the glass, I saw an officer approach my door. Behind him, his arm held by another guard, was a man dressed in the orange scrubs of an inmate. I heard the electronic lock trip and then the officer opened the door ... and in walked a scruffy-looking white adult male, about five-foot-eight and a hundred-and-sixty pounds, with very short hair and this hostile look on his face that said, "Who in the hell are you?" I sized him up as fast as my training allowed—I knew I wasn't going to have much time, and I sure as hell never wanted to come back to this place again. First impressions were all I had to go by, and I was going to have to make them count.

James's facial expression was the first indication of what he may be thinking. Then there was the way he sat down. You see, James didn't sit down so much as he slouched into the seat, his body language broadcasting a challenge with every move. He was determined to hold back what I wanted to know—I could read that in the way he held his arms tightly crossed over his chest, his lips clenched just as tight, displaying an attitude that I was not getting anything out of him. He regarded me with one eyebrow raised, his head tilted slightly to the side, in a guarded yet still "I don't give a shit" posture.

When you have been trained in interviewing people, watching their every movement is key to the way you as an interviewer conduct your interview. Sometimes a subject tells much more than he wants to let out just from his movements and posture. I was looking for anything, from gestures as broad as the head shaking *No* while the mouth is lying *Yes,* down to the merest fleeting tic at the corner of an eye at the moment the most painful question is dropped. James, from his facial expression to the way he sat in the seat, indicated silently to me what my opening remark should be. I could take one of two approaches with his type of personality; James's expression and behavior indicated confusion or skepticism or a blend of both. I could either agree with him and feed into those feelings and then offer solutions, or I could man up and cut to the chase and immediately seize control of the dynamic between us. There are pros and cons to both, but knowing the case and the information I was attempting to validate, I decided to go with the subtle approach first.

"James Doe?" He shook his head yes. "I know I'm catching you by surprise, but I have something *very important* to talk to you about." This statement was one that agreed with his expression. I took great care to stress the words, impressing them into his mind the subtext that since the discussion was one of importance, a feeling of importance would transfer to him, a subliminal ego-stroke that would serve to open him up to me. I also needed my first statement to gain his attention, which this did. Now, it was time to introduce myself.

"James, my name is Eric Echols, and I'm a private investigator investigating Joal Henke in reference to a child molestation case." James immediately piped up with the fact that he had not seen Joal in years. Just like that, one/two. I don't know what the deal was with Joal Henke, but I was beginning to notice that the mere mention of his name produced an immediate and heated response from those people who had been close to him—no one came away from knowing him lukewarm. I replied that I knew it had been awhile since then, but that I needed to talk with him about things that perhaps happened when he was younger ... like back when he used to be around Jane and her mother. Of course I used their real names with him—and just as I expected, at the sound of the names, his slouch stiffened. Those names sent a message to James that warmed his iciness toward me. It told him that I knew something about his past and that I spoke with people whom he at one time in his life had an affection toward. Sometimes just by mentioning a name or referring obliquely to some particular incident will lead people to assume you know all of the details, when in fact you are just mentioning the name or the incident— it's their minds that eagerly fill in the blanks you leave them.

Well, I had chosen the right approach—my interview plan worked. Some investigators would have taken the quick road, winding up little or no information and at a hard-won price, too. But despite his hardened exterior and threatening stance, the subtle approach was what James needed. He looked relieved to finally be telling his side of this long-repressed story.

James began his declaration by stating his family was not well off financially and that Joal Henke had kind of taken this poor kid under his wing and taken care of him. James talked about how he really liked Joal because he would take him on family trips and road trips, teach him taekwondo, and take him to tournaments. When I asked James if he had ever seen Joal with another woman besides his first wife, he suddenly looked up straight into my eyes and a relieved little smile came to his face. He stated that yeah, he had, and he began telling just what he had seen and the women he had seen with Joal. And to complicate matters, Joal knew that

James had seen him at his game and that he knew far too much to be so close. According to James, one day when he happened to be alone with Joal, things got creepy. Joal suddenly shifted gears from Mr. Nice Guy to Satan. He got in James's face and threatened him if he told his family what he had seen. Then it was right back to the pleasant suburban dad. The conversation stayed with him.

The threat was one deterrent, but basically, James didn't want to be the one to break the unsavory news to Joal's family. The knowledge would tear that family apart, and he just couldn't do it to Jane and her mom. But finally, Joal's behavior became too flagrant to ignore. There was the ugly possibility that they would find out about it in the worst way, so James decided to take it on himself to deliver the news to Jane. James told her as delicately as he could about it, but he asked her not to tell her mother because Joal had threatened him. I asked James about the threats that were made, but all he stated was that Joal knew martial arts, and he was scared of him at that time. Keep in mind James at that time was about twelve or thirteen years old. James also stated that he heard Joal make perverted comments towards Jane and her friend about their swimsuits at a pool party—comments referring to size of breasts and how they looked, using words of a sexually descriptive nature. At the time those girls were eleven and thirteen years old.

Not having a tape recorder with me, I did not record the interview with James. When I checked in at the entrance, the prison officers had made me take my recording devices back to my vehicle and lock them up. Knowing I needed to get this interview documented, I asked the officer if I could hand James a pen and some paper, and the officer granted my request.

Below is the entire written statement of Mr. James Doe. The statement is typed exactly as it was written out in longhand by James.

*I, James Doe (full name omitted), on July 13, 2009, was spoken to by Eric Echols, private investigator. This interview took place at Valdosta State Prison, Valdosta GA. During the time I knew Joal Henke I saw Mr. Henke being overly friendly, touching and showing affection for Carolyn [last name omitted to protect her identity] several times. I saw Mr. Henke standing between Carolyn's thighs at the taekwondo tournament Mr. Henke had in Ooltewah High School. Mrs. [last name omitted to protect her identity] was driving a Jeep Grand Cherokee. Mr. Henke explained to me in a way if I told Mrs. Henke what happened or what I saw when it was just us guys around I wouldn't be able to go on road trips and tournaments anymore. I remembered telling [Jane] I thought Joal was cheating on her mom but not to say anything because I felt threatened by Joal. I also thought at times Mr. Henke was too friendly and felt or touched his students to often, both boys and girls. One time at a pool party at [Wife #1's sister]'s house, I heard Joal make a perverted comment to Jane and Girl 2 [name omitted to protect her identity], something to do with one of their swimsuits. I was young at that time but I knew his comment wasn't a correct comment to make toward two little girls. This statement is true to the best of my knowledge. No treats or promises were made to me by Eric Echols.*

With this statement, I now had two adults confirming evidence that Joal Henke, as an adult, had demonstrated appallingly inappropriate and illegal behavior toward minors. As I stated before, all verbal accounts about incidents need to be validated or witnessed, and all leads need to be followed until either confirmed or denied. In this case, Wife #1 had stated that her daughter had a "like-hate" relationship with Joal Henke. Jane had reported that Joal did make inappropriate comments about her breasts when she was twelve years old, the first confirmation of Joal's inappropriate behavior toward minors. James stated that Joal made perverted comments toward two young girls at a pool party and also made threats toward him when he was a young boy—the second confirmation of Joal's inappropriate behavior toward minors, with the added unsettling image of the adult Joal looming over the twelve-year-old James, threatening the boy.

Let me address one issue about James. Just because James was a ward of the state did not mean that he was not a valid witness to what happened when he was a young boy. There are those psychiatrists or psychologists who might just say James made bad decisions because he had a troubled or abusive childhood. It could also be argued that James was acting out by rejecting a criminal justice system that had failed him. I know, it sounds like an episode of *Criminal Minds*, but how often truly does a person act out because of the childhood he or she had? I found James to be credible regarding the information he provided. The main fact was that when James had been a young boy he idolized Joal. As seen through James's awestruck young eyes, Joal was a super cool taekwondo master, almost like some heroic cartoon character made real, and James felt very appreciative and privileged that Joal took him on trips. But now, after so many years, to talk about situations James remembered that were not so favorable for his former idol Joal only makes James's information credible. I am sure if James talked to the right psychiatrist or psychologist, more information about his childhood and more intimate details about what he could remember about Joal could be extracted. But I only had the narrow window of opportunity afforded me by the Georgia prison system. When the time was up, it was UP. The guard told us the time was up, and we rose. I looked at James and thanked him for his time and candor. He looked at it dumbly for a moment, as if puzzled by this small, unexpected, human gesture— and then he replied "you are welcome" and then asked how Wife #1 and Jane were doing? I quickly stated they are both doing well. It was more than just words between two men. The look on his face I could tell for James, in his mind at that moment, was a lifeline to his past, to his life outside. I could feel him drawing strength from me, because I showed him respect even though I was a stranger—inner strength he would need in that snake pit he was in. "Thanks, Bro'," he said, the toughness beginning to creep back into his features as he turned to go. Then we were both led in different directions—James, *in*; me, thankfully, *out*.

As I drove north, I turned these new nuggets over in my mind, fitting them into the growing puzzle. From what I had managed to pick up from James in our brief time together, once I cut through the crap and got him talking about Jane and her mom, I didn't detect any deception in him. This is not to say I was taken in, that he was an innocent choir boy. Our boy James Doe was very likely to some degree a criminal and no doubt had committed some crimes in his adult life; but fortunately, the memories I needed to mine his brain for had happened long before his life of crime had begun. The slouching, hostile con had once been a pretty straight kid, a kid with no illegal enterprises to conceal, a kid who had once had enough of a conscience that he tried to protect his friend and her mom from emotional hurt. However wrong he had veered in his life since then, James's story about Joal's philandering had the ring of truth. I decided that from this private investigator's view, the information provided by James would be regarded as credible. For now.

And the information I discovered about Joal Henke was getting uglier and uglier. I got home from Valdosta exhausted. As soon as I got in the house, I hugged and kissed my wife, I showered, had dinner, and tried to just chill and watch TV while drinking a cocktail (Washington Apple). But the case wouldn't let me alone. I went into my office and switched on the computer, intending to put my notes into the *Joal Henke* file, but it was late and I realized I was too muzzy to read my notes from the day's interview. Instead, I absently flipped through the file, clicking past scans of documents and surveillance photos, coming at last to the publicity photo of the go-getting, polished, professional Joal Henke.

For a long, long moment, I stared at the smiling face in the file photo. The facial expression had a calculated look that was designed to exude happy, breezy confidence. Then I held my hand up to the screen, masking off the lower half of the face and focusing my full attention on the eyes. Taken by themselves, Joal Henke's eyes had a sharp, cruel, intent look to them that didn't match his smiling mouth. It could, of course, mean nothing. Still...something in the disconnect between the expression in the eyes and the un-matching expression of the mouth bothered me. In it, I caught the whiff of the classic sociopathic personality.

A sociopath is a person, often male, who is often well liked because of his charm and charisma, but he does not usually care about other people. He always puts himself first and blames others for his actions. He disregards the rules and constantly does not tell the truth without any feelings of guilt. I thought of another point my investigation had uncovered—the pedophilia angle. A pedophile is a person, also often male, who has an abnormal interest in children. He fantasizes acts of engaging in sexual activity with children to achieve sexual excitement and gratification. He usually also has a disconnect going with his moral compass that helps him rationalize that what he's doing to a kid isn't illegal at all, but uplifting and educating. *One hell of a disconnect*, I thought, still unable to consider that angle of the case without feeling a gut reaction of disgust. How someone could feel like screwing around with kids was okay was beyond me, and I felt like one blessed man for that. But still, this case compelled me to consider this, as repugnant as it was.

I began to work Joal into the equation. Joal had been caught cheating on two wives, which indicated a continuing pattern of lies and deception, as well as callously thoughtless behavior toward each of his wives. Tonya's description of Joal as a man was one who always uses his looks to get what he wanted and Jane's characterization of Joal as cocky and arrogant fit the classic sociopath's profile. And to further point out his arrogance, Joal had been ordered by the Tennessee court not to leave Tennessee with his children while the case was still ongoing; but during our investigation, we discovered that Joal violated this order, flouting the law on two occasions. More disturbing was the pattern of behavior with children on the onset of puberty, which was being increasingly supported by testimony by witnesses: how Joal the adult allegedly enjoyed making inappropriate comments with sexual overtones to children about their body parts; how he then threatened to harm a child if he went forward with the truth of his extramarital affairs. Joal was also called a "pervert," I noted. But still... I stared at the smiling face on the screen and tried to fit the evidence so far around it. Could these really be the eyes of a sociopath with pedophiliac tendencies? And how exactly did all of this lead to Joal's ex-wife Tonya being charged with twenty-two counts of child molestation? Somewhere in this mess was a trail of evidence that linked everything together like a big, beautiful, logical flowchart that led from Point A to Point B—and I had to find it.

But not tonight.

Wherever the answers were, they weren't exactly leaping out at me. I knew the truth was there, but I couldn't see it yet in the pieces of the puzzle that I had discovered so far. All I had were possibilities, and I needed something concrete to hang a solid theory on. It was clear I would have to do a lot more investigative digging. I let out a heavy, irritated sigh and turned the computer off for the night, and then I sat there at my desk rubbing my tired eyes, wondering:

Where the hell *did* the truth lie in this whole twisted-up, horrible case?

## JERRY AND KELLI MCDONALD

Of all the alleged victims' families I came in contact with during my investigation, Jerry Virgil McDonald Jr. proved to be the most sincere. I had done my research, and considering all of the players involved on the other side of the legal fence, Jerry McDonald seemed to have it more together than any of the rest. His daughter had been listed as one of the alleged victims, but Jerry wasn't acting as crazy and precipitously as the other parents in the equation, which made me wonder. My investigation had disclosed that he was truly a family man who cared about people, but his reaction wasn't in line with the behavior of an outraged father—rather he seemed to be plodding along as part of this intertwined group, just following along mutely after everyone else's leads. I must admit, Jerry McDonald was a passive and submissive man. But between the horrible gravity of the alleged crime perpetrated against his child and his lukewarm reaction over it, something just didn't add up. It struck me as being highly unusual. Ordinarily a family man in his situation couldn't help but draw on his own righteous anger, especially when he was part of a group. People who share the same motive usually draw off of each other's emotions, and this emotional effect is often enhanced in a crowd. But Jerry's demeanor seemed somewhat lackadaisical, considering the heavy import of the proceedings. I considered an angle: could Jerry's calm, placid behavior indicate that there really had been no molestation going on—that the core of this whole ugly case was nothing but a hollow lie? Could this be the missing link I was looking for? My mind was a whirlwind, a tornado funnel full of thoughts. I stayed up nights pondering my next move. One thing was for sure: I needed to take action, and soon.

Jerry McDonald seemed to be a swell guy. Mrs. Kelli Bernice McDonald, however, was a different story. By Tonya's account, Jerry's wife was mean as the dickens. Kelli was known to be loud and overbearing at times, and from my previous contact with her, I could imagine that the subject had a bit of a Napoleon complex.

I remember the first time I had come in contact with Kelli McDonald. As part of my duties for Slater & King, as I have mentioned previously, I had to effect process services on the individuals who were involved in the civil case *Tonya Craft vs. Joal Henke*. The McDonalds were on that list. Our encounter had taken place at their home in Catoosa County—but the McDonald home was a far cry from the Lamb residence.

The manicured lawns and wide paved driveways gave way to older, rustic spreads, which in turn became open pastureland and then forest. At the end of a long stretch of county twisting road, when I found the dented mailbox with the McDonald's address scrawled on it, I knew I was in the country. The McDonald home sat on a slight hill, the only house on the lonely route. It was an unmanaged-looking home, to be charitable—it was a place which had not been kept up for some years. As I drove up the unpaved gravel driveway, I could see that the yard had not been taken care of for a long time. Untrimmed shrubs had become wild trees. An old child's bike was lying on the ground. That wasn't the only sign that children lived here: patches of the front yard had been battered down to the bare earth as only the energetic play of kids seem to be able to do. Other bikes and fading plastic toys were scattered about, tossed carelessly wherever some child had been when the moment of play had ceased.

Not even a bird was twittering in the trees, I realized as I got out of my car. Then, a noise to my left alerted me, and I turned, ready—and then relaxed as I saw the cause of the sound. The first sign of life was a mangy, undernourished mutt that stirred itself from its nest from a broken down vehicle next to the house. The animal looked at me with an attitude that was timid and fearful yet at the same time pathetically hopeful. I wished like hell I had something edible on me I could toss to the poor thing. I adopted the posture of a friendly human and extended my hand, but the dog miserably cringed away from me with its tail tucked between its legs and vanished behind the house.

I walked across the yard to the front door. The place had gone to seed, but here and there among the overgrowth and litter, I could see the telltale signs of good intentions somehow thwarted just short of completion and left to the elements. An old vehicle, its hood yawning open, sat out in the side yard next to the house, looking as if someone at some time had been trying to fix it—but the reality was more likely that by now the rusting hulk was little more than a home for stray cats.

The whole lost, sad atmosphere of the McDonald's home had a creepy surrealistic feel to it. The lonely desolation of the yard and the house reminded me of the home in *Misery*; I found myself idly wondering if Kathy Bates were waiting behind the front door, all tricked out like the psychopath Annie Wilkes with a log of firewood in her hands, waiting to get the drop on me...! *I gotta stop watching all those movies!*

I walked up the steps, noting that there was a mess of clutter and trash on the porch to match the yard. I imagined that the inside décor continued this dreary theme of decay and despair. As I knocked on the door, I could hear the approaching patter of little bare feet coming closer and children's voices saying excitedly, "Someone's at the door!" I would imagine that for them, living here at the end of this road to nowhere, a visitor would be like a treat.

The knob turned and the door creaked open, and there stood Jerry and Kelli McDonald. Jerry, smiling obligingly, looked like your everyday easygoing country guy. The short, rather stocky woman beside him wasn't exactly what I expected. She had highlighted blond hair that was cut in a style that looked to be too high-tone for the environment she was living in. I was looking for someone a little more homely, and this looked like that was not the case. "Mister and Mrs. McDonald?" I asked, and smiled. Jerry nodded and replied yes. But Kelli, on the other hand, for all her acquired polish, wasn't about to play the paragon of rural Southern hospitality.

"Who are you?!" Kelli McDonald demanded, all attitude, her face twisted and teeth almost bared. There went any degree of attractiveness the woman had. In Kelli McDonald's voice I could detect the familiar traces of a vocal tone I'd heard over and over on a certain videotape. That little trait totally fit into the profile I had drawn up: the group dynamic at work here was as clear as a flowchart.

Let's face it—Kelli was a very close friend of Sandra Lamb. Although Kelli could sometimes be aggressive, basically she was more of a follower than a leader and seemed to fall easily under the influence of the domineering Sandra. Looking at the behavior of Kelli and knowing the type of behavior Sandra Lamb often displayed, I could see the classic pattern of the high-school social pack: You know, that person in school who chooses the wrong friends, runs with a fast crowd, and wants to be just like the leader of the pack, the alpha female? This alpha girl's family has money, clout, and influence, but the beta girl's doesn't. So the follower adapts by developing protective coloration; she shapes her persona to emulate the alpha, knowing that as long as she strokes the leader's ego and mimics her, she will acquire financial and social benefits from the association. My grandmother used to call it "riding someone else's coattail." There was a whole lot of that going on here, and it was muddying the water way too much.

Jerry was polite and accepting, but Kelli was hostile and snappish—not nearly as unbridled and bigoted as Sandra had been, but I could tell that if Kelli McDonald really got wound up, she'd go off loud and long. Perhaps her placid husband's energy helped keep one foot on her brake. Anyhow, I was just glad this go-round wasn't like my encounter with Sandra; at least I wasn't getting physically assaulted and then called something even uglier for simply performing my duty as an officer of the court. I served the papers to Jerry and Kelli McDonald, said goodbye, and left.

In the time since that encounter, I had thought back a few times to Jerry McDonald, the pleasant fellow who politely stood in his doorway and accepted like an upright man the legal papers I had had to serve him. From what I was learning about this little Southern-fried clique, he seemed like the only real, living human being on that whole side of the equation. Everyone else seemed to be hiding behind some sort of mask, and when those masks slipped, things could get ugly fast. But there was something about Jerry that I thought I could reach—if I only had a chance. But how?

I knew that if I went to Jerry's residence to attempt an interview, Kelli would see that I didn't get the opportunity. She'd prevent our meeting, plus I had no doubt that she'd probably put her foot down right then and there and read poor Jerry the riot act about me—and that perfect window of opportunity would totally slam shut, right in my face. This is why doing your homework on the key players in any case is paramount to the outcome and what you as a private investigator want to accomplish. With Jerry being as henpecked as he was, I did not want to risk the chance of Kelli raising holy hell at home about him talking to me. My belief was that Jerry would talk to me if we were alone—and as long as his wife did not know. My best option was to contact him where he worked.

You can sometimes tell what kind of person someone is by the career he or she has chosen. People who become doctors or other players in the medical field are motivated by a strong desire to help other people. Likewise, often someone will become a police officer to protect people from harm. An American serviceman such as a Marine is someone who defends the country, fighting for the rights of others. These occupations take more than motivation: they take passion, dedication, and total commitment to the cause, whether it's defending a nation in a strange, foreign land or standing out in the rain at 3 a.m. on a country road soothing some scared, broken, bleeding kid who's pinned in a wrecked car while the rescue crew does their thing with the Jaws of Life. People who place themselves on the frontlines in the service of their fellow human beings are the salt of the earth to me.

Jerry McDonald, bless him, was one of those people who felt that call to serve. He had a strong background in care-giving and protecting the well-being of others. Jerry had worked at Hamilton County EMS and then American Medical Response as a licensed paramedic. When I located him, he was working for LifeForce, an emergency-response helicopter unit based out of Chattanooga whose main purpose is to save lives.

Finding out this information about Jerry was important: the career he had chosen suggested that he possessed a powerful degree of compassion—and to boot, he was a good old country boy. Not to mention that my research had uncovered the fact that Jerry himself had been a victim of molestation when he was younger, which gave him a unique perspective on the whole issue. This inside information I had, coupled with the understanding of the type of person Jerry McDonald was, made it very easy to narrow down my choice of which of the prosecution's main witnesses I thought would talk to me. My professional instinct, that gut feeling I always get when something good is about to happen, was telling me, "Eric, go talk to Jerry McDonald." There was something about him that didn't add up, and my gut wouldn't let me be over that unsettling detail; Jerry's behavior was not consistent with the rest of the pack. In cases like this one—or really any other criminal case, when I get down to it—sometimes all I have is my gut. Those feelings come on so strong sometimes that they must be followed, and the track record I've racked up playing my hunches and following my instincts have paid off so richly in the past that I have to pay attention to them. So my decision to speak with Jerry Virgil McDonald Jr. was a gimme.

My assessment of Jerry was that if I had the opportunity to talk to him as one man to another and came out and asked him if it was possible that his daughter had not been molested in any way, he would tell me straight because Jerry was by nature, or at least the nature of his career, a care provider and a nurturer. As an interviewer, having someone like this to interview was a blessing in waiting, not only because of his profession but because of his helpful nature. Jerry was a person who could provide valuable facts and information in the Tonya Craft case. He could be my ace in the hole.

One of the key points when interviewing is to conduct the interview in a location where the interviewer can maintain a level of control. Normally, you would not allow for the interviewee to select the location, because the last thing you want is for your subject to be answering your questions in a situation where he would be in familiar surroundings, relaxed, comfortable, and most of all in control. Why do you think the police always conduct their interviews at the police station? Had this been the type of interview that was more of an interrogation, one in which the interviewee was a suspect, the interviewer would select a location where the subject would feel awkwardly out of place, uncomfortable, and out of control from the get-go. That would be the gameplan—normally. However, this wasn't a case of intimidating a perp in a police station. From all reports and from what I had seen of him in our brief prior contact, Jerry McDonald appeared to be an upright, honest man, and I was going to treat him as such. By this I mean that I would be friendly, not pushy; I would take my time and show this man the consideration and compassion he deserved. Above all, I knew that if this plan had a chance of working, Jerry needed to feel he could trust me if he were going to open up to me to any degree.

LifeForce, the medevac helicopter service where Jerry was presently employed in Chattanooga, Tennessee, was a 24/7 operation located up on the roof of a medical building in the downtown area. I called LifeForce and asked for Jerry McDonald to see if I could get his work schedule. I had learned through research and investigation techniques that Jerry was part of the night crew, so I timed my interview with him when his shift was just starting so that he would be fresh.

On July 15, 2009, I drove to Chattanooga, and by 8:30 p.m., I was striding into the building where LifeForce was based. I took the elevator up to its offices on the top floor. As I left the elevator and strolled up to the company's door, out of habit, I noticed every detail I could as fast as possible: The battered steel door had a small chicken-wired glass window and a card-key reader. An intercom call box was on the wall beside the door. The standard wall-mounted CCTV surveillance camera with its blinking red eye was bracketed up high on the wall, set off a bit to the side. I was glad I had called ahead. I had anticipated this degree of security—anything less than that was foolish in this day and age. I know I'd sure want to get a look at who was approaching my door if I had a helicopter full of fuel on top of a building right downtown. I noticed that the surveillance camera was positioned mainly to give a clear shot of any and all visitors as they exited the elevators and approached the door.

I pushed the button on the call box. When a voice came on, I identified myself. "Hey there, I'm Eric Echols—I'm here to see Jerry McDonald?" I let my voice rise up into a question, giving my request a casual, offhand tone. I took a step back, looked up, and smiled helpfully into the lens. As I turned toward the door with my back to the camera, I surreptitiously hit the *record* button on my recording device in my left breast shirt pocket. I heard the electronic lock click, and the door opened. I walked in, and Jerry McDonald met me in the hall.

"Hey, man," I said gently and smiled as I extended my hand to him to shake his hand, showing respect and friendliness.

"How you doing?" he replied. Jerry hid any confusion on his part under his good Southern manners.

I wanted the ID to be clear on the tape. "Jerry?" I asked. He responded with a "Yeah," and I continued. "I'm Eric Echols."

"Nice to meet you." Jerry McDonald was a totally average man, unassuming and soft-spoken, and his accent carried a lazy drawl that fit his easygoing demeanor.

"We met before," I told him, to help jog his memory, but to this, he again responded in agreement with an "All right," even though I was sure he didn't recall our previous encounter and had forgotten that he had seen me at his home when I effected the process service. "You might not remember me," I said helpfully. "I'm a private investigator on the Tonya Craft case."

"Uh huh," Jerry said. Then he and I looked at each other for an awkward moment, standing there in the foyer.

Keep in my mind that my objective was to see if Jerry would talk to me and provide any information that would aid in the investigation I was conducting on behalf of Tonya. Knowing that his daughter was one of the alleged victims, I expected Jerry to tell me to get the [*expletive deleted*] out of there. As respectful and caring as I thought Jerry was, I was still only making an assumption as to what I thought Jerry would say. On the other hand, taking a wild leap is often part and parcel of a PI's strategy; if I conducted investigations based on what I expected might happen or what I thought people would say, then I would hardly ever resolve a case. My rule of thumb is to expect the unexpected and to never assume—because as we all know, when you ASSUME, you make an ASS out of U and ME.

The unexpected is exactly what unfolded—in more ways than one. At least I was prepared for what happened with the interview.

Despite my previous concern to the contrary, in the short time it took to meet the man, I could tell that Jerry McDonald was going to be a good interview subject. His automatic answers in the affirmative, even while giving little information, were still like a barometer of his willingness to please a questioner. It's a behavior pattern that submissive personalities display, and Jerry was proving to be true to form. But this sort of conversation was too delicate to take place there, exposed in the foyer.

I gave him a look of concern and gestured toward the interior of the LifeForce offices. "You want to talk in private?" I asked him, and Jerry led me down the corridor to an empty lounge area that had a couch, some chairs, and a table. We sat down.

On a side note, if you want to be a good interviewer, you need to prepare what you are going to say at the first opportunity you engage in the conversation. I teach my students that the success of the interview depends on the interviewer's abilities and skills. Successful interviewers must exude self-confidence and professionalism in appearance and demeanor. Interviews are the most critical stage of an investigation because they are the primary source of information. In a 2007 article that I wrote for the *CFI Insider: A Journal for the Certified Forensic Interviewer*, titled "From a Private Investigator's Perspective: Conducting Dishonest Employee Interviews," I discuss the strategic importance of the introduction phase of any type of interview:

> "This is where it all begins, with the initial contact between the interviewer and the interviewee. As in a boxing match, you're in one corner and your opponent is in the other. When you both approach the center of the ring, you are eye to eye, and the next thing you hear is the bell signaling that it's time to come out and fight. You both dance and throw jabs, hooks, overhand rights, and uppercuts. As an interviewer, the first thing you must do is take control. Throw the first jab by controlling the introduction."

I had done my research and honed an approach that was tailored to Jerry's particular personality type. I couldn't take the hard-edged approach. While Jerry, being such a tractable type, would probably respond to that tactic to some degree, in the long run it wouldn't pay off. The likelihood was that he'd clench up and get nervous enough to hold back information which he'd otherwise offer up willingly. No, that wouldn't work—this was a man for whom an emotional appeal would work the best. In my personal introduction to Jerry at the outset of the interview, I needed to build credibility in my investigation so that he would believe in the investigation. My technique was to quickly identify who I was and capture his attention, while at the same time showing him respect. Mutual respect was paramount, because I needed to show him I could be trusted enough for him to talk to me.

The initial exchange you have read between Jerry McDonald and me when we first met is taken from that surveillance tape I had running; the words are verbatim, just as they were spoken, without additions or omissions. This part of my story is a direct transcription from that tape. Here is the introduction I used with Jerry McDonald:

**ERIC ECHOLS:** Yeah. Just want to talk to you in private. I—I've been doing an investigation, and I'm sure—surrounding a bunch of things with—involving you and—and your past and with your daughter.

**JERRY McDONALD:** Uh huh.

**ECHOLS:** I've talked to—I don't know if your dad told you. I came by there and talked to him, talked to your dad and your mom. And I just kind of wanted to sit down here and talk to you and see if you'd spend some time in talking to me kind of about your past and what's going on with your daughter. From my investigation, I know that you're a pretty reasonable guy.

**McDONALD:** Right.

**ECHOLS:** And I know a lot of times things happen where people get forced or they just have an opportunity not to say something at a particular time and they keep quiet, you know, dealing with child molestation and things of that nature or just the accusation of child molestation. And then—you know, I've been doing this investigation for quite some time now, and the only thing I can do is come to a person who I think is honest. That's why I tracked down your dad, and I went by them and, you know, they didn't want to talk about your past when you were molested. They wanted me to talk to you directly about that, which is fine, but also, the things that happened with your daughter and the cousin, [*name of minor child omitted*]. There were some inappropriate things that they've done. And I'm finding all these things out in the investigation, and I'm going to have to be, you know, honest with you, man. I'd rather come and talk to you because enough is enough. We need to put all these false allegations behind. And the only way that this is really going to happen is come to a person like yourself and see what we can do to—to resolve this whole issue. So that's why I'm here. I'm here to talk to you about that and about the allegations against Tonya Craft, which those are false allegations as well. And, you know, just looking you in your eyes and talking to you and knowing the type of person that you are, I came to you man-to-man. That's why I'm here. So where do you want to begin? I mean, I'm coming to you straight, man. Coming to you straight. I don't want to bring in any past with your family. I don't want to draw—you know, draw that out into court or anything of that nature.

**McDONALD:** What do you mean by that?

**ECHOLS:** As far as—as far as having, you know, just—just the whole ordeal about you and your ordeal when you were a child. Like I told your parents, you know, a lot of times when you go back into the past, that brings out a lot of open wounds that have already been closed—people have moved on. But, you know, again, we're looking at these false allegations against Tonya. And I'm going to be honest with you. Through my investigation there's no way in the world I— that those things happened with your daughter. You know it, I know it, but no one's saying it. And I'm going to be honest with you, man, I can't figure out why. I can't figure out why no one's come to court— you know what, this is bullshit, enough is enough.

As you can see in my introduction to Jerry, I identified myself and built credibility in my investigation by stating I knew about personal occurrences that happened to him and with his daughter and a cousin, a lead-in that certainly captured his attention. I showed Jerry respect as well as earned his respect by telling him he was a "pretty reasonable guy" and that I came to him because he was honest. Then, I cut to the chase for him by stating:

**ECHOLS:** I've been doing an investigation, and I'm sure—surrounding a bunch of things with—involving you and—and your past and with your daughter.

This was a vague comment, one that didn't come right out and identify any specifics but which strongly implied that he and I had something to talk about. Jerry's response was one of agreement. I studied the way he reacted and I detected no nonverbal denials, so I continued. I next mentioned talking to his parents. The reason I mentioned it was an attempt to build a rapport between us and add some creditability for myself and my investigation. I wanted Jerry to feel that if his parents spoke to me, it was OK for him to speak to me. Then I provided him with a few possible reasons as to why he never came forward when he was molested, and I stated the following:

**ECHOLS:** And I know a lot of times things happen where people get forced or they just have an opportunity not to say something at a particular time and they keep quiet, you know, dealing with child molestation and things of that nature or just the accusation of child molestation.

As you can see, here I spoke more directly to Jerry about the nature of the case, as well as providing him with a theory as to why people don't come forward when there is an implication or act of molestation. I was looking to get a verbal reaction out of Jerry while all the time reading his body language. At this point, I was prepared for some sort of a denial, verbal or nonverbal—but Jerry did not present one. As a matter fact, he just sat there and listened. Jerry's reaction indicated to me he was becoming more submissive and, as an interviewer, that is what one looks for in an interviewee. For example, in a standard dishonest-employee type of interview, an attitude of submission shows that the person is caving in and is getting ready to confess to the crime. In this case, I read it as Jerry wanting to talk. But remember my prizefighter analogy about the introduction stage of interviewing? Even though this was a friendly discussion between Jerry and me, on another level, a structural level, this exchange was like a boxing match, So far with my questions I had thrown a jab or two. What was also happening was that as I asked him every succeeding question, I was drawing further into the heart of the matter. With each step, I got more specific about allegations, directing more comments specifically toward Jerry. I could tell he was receiving my message loud and clear, because his body language remained submissive and he did not display any physical signs to indicate to me that I was veering off track. I was looking for the private investigator's textbook signs of skeptical suspicion: a cocked head with a little narrowing at the corners of his eyes, tightened lips, discolor creeping into his face. Jerry showed no signs of this. He remained receptive. Not seeing any negative, blocking reactions from him, I decided to forge on ahead, so I stated the following:

> **ECHOLS:** And I'm finding all these things out in the investigation, and I'm going to have to be, you know, honest with you, man. I'd rather come and talk to you because enough is enough. We need to put all these false allegations behind. And the only way that this is really going to happen is come to a person like yourself and see what we can do to—to resolve this whole issue.

And...nothing. No body language stop signs from Jerry McDonald, and I know the signs like I know the alphabet, and from both extremes and in between. I know how to talk to a subject and at the same time read that person's every move, beginning with his general overall appearance; whether he looks me in the eye or tries to avoid my gaze during the interview; if his posture is noticeably tense and upright with him perched on the edge of his seat, or if it is way too relaxed, with the subject sometimes looking almost prone in the chair as if broadcasting his complete and total lack of concern with the topic at hand; listening to note how often he might move his legs underneath the table; any sort of tapping or fidgeting or other repetitive nervous signal; what certain talking points cause an almost imperceptible movement or clearing of the throat—all the way to the opposite extreme, like when the subject is just sitting there with a frozen affect, not moving at all, looking down at his hands on the table in front of him as if to see if the blood is leaving his fingertips—these are all just some of the things an interviewer looks for to decide whether and when to make a direct accusation. After making a few soft accusations as to what I was there to talk about and still not getting any indication from Jerry in the form of a denial, I took Jerry's receptive silence and continued submissiveness as signs that he was in agreement with me and that he himself believed what I was saying was true. So I got more direct. I stated the following:

> **ECHOLS:** So that's why I'm here. I'm here to talk to you about that and about the allegations against Tonya Craft, which those are false allegations as well.

This was all done in the first few minutes that passed from the time Jerry and I said hello at the front door. Now, I directly stated that I was there to talk about my client Tonya Craft and that the allegations against her were false. On hearing the one-two punch of the accused name and the statement that their claims were false, any person who truly believed that his daughter had been molested by that person would have reacted in some way, from a terse, measured disagreement all the way to an emotional outburst. In fact, as he sat there silently looking back at me, I noticed moisture beginning to well up in Jerry's eyes. He appeared to be getting teary-eyed, which is certainly not a sign of disagreement—it's more of a sign of sorrow, of regrets or the releasing of guilt. We sat there for a moment, saying nothing, and my heart went out to this poor, tormented guy. His heart was heavy with baggage that had weighed on him almost all his life, and right now, he was wrapping his mind around the possibility that this was the moment when he could let go of all of that pain, that burden he had silently borne all these years... Jerry McDonald, his soul yearning for some sort of absolution, was teetering on the edge of a pivotal moment in his life. I could tell that his shoulders were shaking almost imperceptibly. I leaned forward, just slightly, not invading his space yet still presenting myself as a rock, a figure of gentle strength and support. I looked at him unblinkingly, openly, and spoke again:

> **ECHOLS:** And, you know, just looking you in your eyes and talking to you and knowing the type of person that you are, I came to you man to man. That's why I'm here.

By that point Jerry's tears were about to overflow, and I could tell that he was about to cry. There is nothing wrong with a man crying. Just put in the movie "Rudy" and when the part comes up where the coach finally puts Rudy in the game and he sacks the quarterback—yes, you will see me cry. Jerry's tears indicated to me that this meek, quiet man had a lot to say, and it was ready to come out. While I felt for what Jerry McDonald was going through, I still had a professional purpose for this exchange. This was an interview, and I needed to conduct it not from an emotional standpoint, but as a methodical investigator. I let my comment sink in, then I started rationalizing with Jerry to get him to talk so I could see what he wanted to say. Rationalizations during the course of an interview can be tricky, because I had to do a tightrope walk: the interviewer needs to show *empathy* without showing *sympathy*. In this case, I needed to convey to Jerry that I understood as a father why a person in his position had not come forward with the fact that he did not believe Tonya Craft was guilty, while at the same time not showing him sympathy for not having come forward by now to clear Tonya's name. My rationalization was not meant to reopen old wounds from when Jerry was a child—but when I addressed his own molestation, it awakened that suppressed pain. The fact that he didn't have to hide that from me, that horrible heavy secret he had carried for most of his life, was an opportunity for Jerry to finally get some understanding, some closure. During this phase of our exchange, Jerry had asked me what I meant, but he never became upset, nor did he show any animosity toward me.

Looking into Jerry's welling eyes, I was thinking that if there was a time to throw an overhand right, the knockout punch, it was now. I threw the punch by stating this:

> **ECHOLS:** But, you know, again, we're looking at these false allegations against Tonya. And I'm going to be honest with you. Through my investigation there's no way in the world I—that those things happened with your daughter. You know it, I know it, but no one's saying it. And I'm going to be honest with you, man, I can't

figure out why. I can't figure out why no one's come to court—you know what, this is bullshit. Enough is enough.

Under normal circumstances, an interviewer will never make a direct accusation in the introduction—at least, that is the case in a routine dishonest-employee interview. But this interview was much bigger than resolving a dishonest-employee theft case. The stakes were very high, and I knew Tonya Craft's life was on the razor's edge here. I knew that with an innocent woman's life hanging in the balance, I had to make a gutsy move—and based on reading the behavior and body language of Jerry and the fact that he never showed any form of denials, verbal or nonverbal, I just came out and laid it on the line by stating that not only were the allegations against Tonya Henke Craft false, but through my investigation it had become clear that there was no way in the world his daughter had been molested—that I knew it and he, father of one of the alleged victims, knew it.

Now I have to say, at this point, I was expecting Jerry to snap, to jump up and tell me to get out. I even expected Jerry to tell me to go to hell on a locomotive. But Jerry did nothing of the sort. He remained sitting in the same position as he had been when I began talking to him, and we just kept talking. His tone of voice stayed low; he did not even address what I had said. But once the unspoken secret had been spoken out loud, it unleashed a flow of words from this long-suffering man. For over an hour and a half, Jerry McDonald poured out his soul, and what he told me moved me to pity. He was a good man, and he didn't deserve what happened to him back then. Hell, no kid does.

Below is a summary of what Jerry stated in our first interview.

1. Jerry admitted he was molested as a child, and that his wife found a suicide letter that he was going to kill himself due to the memories of the molestation.

2. Jerry stated that his wife told him about an awkward sex-play situation that had been discovered between his young daughter and her female cousin. Jerry was told his daughter and the other girl were just looking at each inappropriately. Jerry did not know when the incident had occurred.

3. Jerry stated he told the DA, Chris Arnt, that he and his family did not want to be involved in the Craft case and that the DA told Jerry he had to be involved in it . At one point, Jerry stated he was being forced by the DA.

4. Jerry stated that he was not aware he could get help from outside counsel to get him and his family out of the Craft case.

5. Jerry stated that his wife took their daughter to their own family doctor, who told them their daughter showed NO physical evidence of molestation.

6. Jerry stated that his daughter was examined twice, once by the family doctor and once by the SANE (Sexual Assault Nurse Examiner) on duty.

7. Jerry stated after his doctor told them there was no evidence, he called the DA and told him what their doctor stated and informed Arnt that they did not want to be involved in the Craft Case.

8. Jerry stated he has only been letting this go on because he felt he was being forced by the DA. He did not have any money to get counsel for his family and was not aware he had any other options.

9. Jerry stated that he never asked his daughter what, if anything, had happened.

10. Jerry stated he thought about how Tonya Craft was doing and that he loved Tonya Craft as a sister.

To get the full gist of the interview I had with Jerry McDonald, you would need to read the entire transcript and listen to the audio recording, dated July 15, 2009. I have, however, compiled a synopsis of the transcript highlighting important facts of the exchange between us.

## Synopsis of Transcript from Audio Dated July 15, 2009

Page and
Line Number

| | |
|---|---|
| 14: 1 -25 | Jerry McDonald (JM) stated he did not want to be a part of the case. |
| 20:8 | JM stated he did not want to be a part of the case. |
| 24: 7 – 30: 13 | JM talked more about how the DA gave him and his wife no choice and they wanted out of the case. |
| 32:4 – 33:19 | JM talked about that he wanted out of this case and agreed to get his story out. |
| 35:1-3 | JM stated he did not want to be a part of the case (Tonya Craft case). |
| 35:11- 36:6 | JM asked what he and his wife could do to get out of the case, and I replied to find representation. |
| 37:2 – 8 | I suggested to Jerry to call an attorney. |
| 38:25 – 39:3 | JM stated his daughter is a good girl and does not lie, then JM stated that all kids lie. |
| 40:5- 44:21 | JM admitted to daughter and cousin looking at each other's privates. |

| | |
|---|---|
| 43:1 – 5 | JM stated that he and his wife were pulled into it (Tonya Craft case). |
| 45:1 – 46:17 | I asked if I could to talk to his daughter with consent from JM and his wife. |
| 47:23 – 48:23 | JM stated he got a letter from the DA directing him not to talk to Tonya's attorneys or investigator. Again I suggested he should talk to someone. |
| 48:24 – 49:25 | JM expressed concern for Tonya Craft. |
| 50:21-25 | I suggested talking to someone in the legal field to learn his options. |
| 51:5 – 25 | I asked about talking to wife and child, only if wife agrees. |
| 52:1 | I attempted to leave the interview and JM asked, "But you still think we can get out of it?" I stayed and continued talking to JM. |
| 52:3 – 53:25 | JM asked me how he can get out of the case and I stated he needed to call an attorney. JM stated the DA forced his hand and that DA made them be in the Craft case. |
| 56:13 | JM stated that he appreciated me coming to see him. |
| 58:9 – 21 | JM stated he did not have money for an attorney; I replied that there are programs out there to assist with attorney fees. |
| 63:22 | JM stated how "it's been nice talking" to me. |
| 64:9 | As I was walking out of the interview, JM asked me to come back and talk some more. |
| 65:3 -21 | JM talked about when he was abused. |
| 68:12 – 72:13 | JM talked about taking his daughter to their family doctor and their doctor stating there was no physical evidence of molestation. JM stated that's when he called the DA and wanted out of the case. I replied he needed to talk to an attorney. |

| | |
|---|---|
| 72:14 – 73:11 | I talked about how the allegations were ruining Tonya Craft's life, what can happen civilly, and the difference between criminal and civil cases. |
| 73:25 – 76:19 | JM questioned if he called an attorney could the DA still make him participate in the case. JM stated he feels like the victim. I suggested getting help from an attorney who could answer his concerns. |
| 77:24 – 79-25 | I explained "witch hunt" and talked about JM's doctor stating there was no sign of penetration in the daughter. JM also mentioned being strong-armed by the DA; JM replied that he was shocked when he was told by the DA his family was still a part of the case though they did not want to be. |
| 86:9 – 89:2 | I explained CFI as being a Certified Forensic Interviewer— trained to conduct interviews in all situations. I also stated that I could not teach someone in twenty minutes how to conduct interviews with someone. I asked to talk to JM's wife. JM replied he would ask his wife, but could not make any promises. |
| 89:23 – 90:24 | I stated I could not give legal advice and that I could only advise him to call an attorney. |
| 95:13 – 99:2 | JM and I talked about riding our motorcycles, camping, and where we liked to go when we take vacations. |
| 104:10 – 105:20 | JM and I talked about church and the ministries I was involved with. JM stated he was fine after our conversation ended. |
| 106:9 - 22 | I stated I had been out all day tracking down leads and witnesses. JM replied, "On the hunting trail"; I laughed and agreed. JM acknowledged he would let me know what his wife said about interviewing her and the daughter. JM stated that it was nice meeting me. |

This synopsis was developed from the audio recording and transcript of the audio recording by a professional court-approved transcriber. Our conversation was willing, nonthreatening, and non-confrontational. It had been a good, productive interview, to say the least, and that's an understatement. This one discussion was going to blow the lid off of this entire case against Tonya Craft. But above and beyond that consideration, there was something more.

This man Jerry McDonald had managed to put a sympathetic face on Ringgold, Georgia, for me. I had been accepting the twisted, hateful mask of Sandra Lamb as being the norm for the rest of Catoosa County. Her spite and ugliness had given me the sour impression that this mountain town was a place where the clocks had stopped in the middle of a 1930s Klan rally. In 98 minutes and change, however, Jerry McDonald had turned all of that around and shown me that there was a side of that place where people had some values, compassion, and common decency.

And above all, Jerry McDonald was a decent man. You could tell he grew up calling his elders *sir* or *ma'am*. By no means is there anything wrong with that, because I do the same—it's called respect! But the full-on respect that Jerry McDonald gave everyone in the world around him was something as rare as finding an honest man—which I could tell that Jerry also was. He embodied the image of the virtuous country boy to the *nth* degree. Jerry could have been a character on some classic family television show like "Little House on the Prairie" or "The Andy Griffith Show." He was a solid, upright man who was unafraid to be exactly what he was, no more, no less: a mama's boy with good, old-fashioned morals, Mr. Ingalls meets Andy Taylor—that was Jerry McDonald. I had thought they didn't make 'em that foursquare and upright anymore, but meeting this one man opened my eyes and balanced the bad impression I was getting about Catoosa County as a whole.

As I walked out the LifeForce building, I had a deep feeling of accomplishment and relief that my gut instinct about Jerry had been right on point. More so, after this interview, I knew within myself that Tonya had been telling the truth after all. She had been straight up with me all along; she was indeed innocent.

I was relieved to feel my doubts about Tonya Craft begin to dissolve. As long as I've been an investigator, there is always something that holds me back from complete and total belief in a subject—even when it's the person who has hired me. It's not that I don't want to trust them; it's that I can't allow myself to, not if I'm going to be an effective investigator for them. I'm sure it's been frustrating for some of my clients that the PI who's working on their cases is also their biggest skeptic—but it's for their own good, and mine, too. Everyone has secrets, some heavier than others, and there's always an outside chance that some ugly fact a client has managed to keep hidden from me could come back and bite both of us on the ass right at the wrong time. I had almost begun to expect it, the ol' late-in-the-game standard confession of "Oh, yeah, um, I forgot this one little absolutely freaking *crucial* detail..."—not because I was cold toward my fellow man, but from tried experience.

At that point, as I slid into the Caddy and fastened myself in to head back to The LPS Group offices to update the files, I knew the game had changed. This was the break we'd been looking for. Tonya Henke Craft was going to be acquitted, and I knew I had to be ready when the time came for me to testify as to what role my investigation played. I had every confidence in the outcome, because what Jerry told me shot the holy hell out of the DA's case. I couldn't wait to drop that bombshell in court. The looks on one side of the courtroom were going to be priceless.

When I met her, Tonya Craft had been up to her eyeballs in ugliness and protesting her innocence. I had wanted to take her at her word—but at the same time, I recognized that maybe that was simply because I wanted this whole horrible thing to not be true. I hadn't expected to be so struck by the details of this case, but it was like a kick in the gut. I was used to the horrors human beings visit on one another. I had seen enough as a Marine and an investigator to prove me to be one hardened professional. But once this case was all drawn out for me, with all the horrible details and case studies and variations and cold, clinical language—I wanted to do nothing but shut it all out, erase it, deny that this kind of hideous, brutal evil could even exist in the world, let alone in the form of a person whose life goal was nurturing and guiding and teaching children. But that's the kind of thinking that can cloud your judgment. So I had been a hard-ass sometimes on the poor woman along the way. Even when my investigation found evidence that corroborated Tonya's version of events or a new level of twisted intrigue revealed itself, part of me kept doubting her.

But now I could finally give my client that last degree of confidence I had withheld. And she in turn was going to be able to think of herself as a free woman.

Looking back on things, I should have been worrying about *my* future as a free man. No good deed goes unpunished, they say— and while Jerry McDonald and I had attained a measure of mutual respect, I sure as hell didn't have a female fan club up in Catoosa County. It didn't take long at all for the crap to hit the fan, and when it did, it hit big—but it took its sweet time hitting *me*.

# THUNDER ON THE SOUNDTRACK

I was feeling so positive about the way my interview with Jerry McDonald had played out that I didn't give any thought to what was going to transpire in Ringgold. Thinking about it later, I could see how the sequence probably played out: Kelli McDonald is a good friend of Sandra Lamb. I show up working on Tonya Craft's team, with Sandra and Kelli on the other side of the fence. Jerry lets slip to his wife Kelli that he's spoken to me, Tonya's private investigator. Kelli freaks out at the news, and chances are good her first move is to get on the horn to tell her good friend Sandra all about it. I'm not saying this in speculation or because of what I learned about Kelli during my investigation, but based on Kelli McDonald's testimony given during the Tonya Craft trial. This information came to light during the cross examination of Kelli by Clancy Covert, one of the attorneys on Tonya's defense team— testimony that you can read here:

**COVERT:** Your husband's name is Jerry, I think you said.

**KELLI McDONALD:** Correct.

**COVERT:** Okay. Jerry talked to my private investigator, Eric Echols, at one point, correct?

**McDONALD:** Yes.

**COVERT:** Okay. And you got mad at him, right?

**McDONALD:** Yes, I did.

**COVERT:** Okay. You told him that you were told not to talk to anyone helping Tonya; is that right?

**McDONALD:** Yes.

**COVERT:** Who told you that?

**McDONALD:** No, nobody told me that. I just told him that he did not need to be talking to anyone that was helping her.

**COVERT:** Did you tell—did you tell Jerry that either the detectives or the DA's office told you not to talk to anyone helping Tonya?

**McDONALD:** I don't recall.

**COVERT:** Okay. Is that possible you told him that?

**McDONALD:** It could be.


As you read this part of Kelli McDonald's testimony, you will notice that when she was asked on the stand whether she told her husband that she was advised not to talk to anyone who was helping Tonya Craft, Kelli first answered, "Yes," to that question— a "Yes" response that was direct, unwavering, and without doubt. But when the question got more specific and she was asked who told her, Kelli McDonald became vague, trying to double back and swear that no, nobody told her—out of her own volition, she told her husband he didn't need to be talking to anyone that was helping her (referring to Tonya Craft). Then the final waffling response as Kelli was asked a direct question as to whether either the detectives or the DA's office told her not to talk to anyone helping Tonya. Kelli then replied, "I don't recall."

*"I don't recall."* That old trick again.

You've already heard my professional opinion on the "I don't recall" game—how the phrase "I don't recall" is the classic weasel's response, a back-out evasive non-answer people give when asked a question they know the answer to but don't want to *really* answer it. The red-flag response "I don't recall" is often used by someone wanting to protect another person—or trying to create some comfortable distance between themselves and the incident.

Whether the subject is a uniformed employee being interrogated in a corporate interviewing room or a witness sitting on the stand giving testimony in a criminal trial, the same human mechanics are at work. The same patterns of evasion and misinterpretation pop up time and time again, and Kelli wasn't creative enough to put a new spin on the old tried-and-tried-again trick of "I don't recall."

Yeah, of course she didn't recall—it was a perfect escape hatch for the prosecuting attorney's and her if they needed to change their game plan in mid-play. Then, later, if Kelli were forced to take the stand due to a civil suit and was asked again, "Did the detectives or the DA's office tell you not to talk to anyone helping Tonya Craft?"— and then if some form of proof like a letter or recording were presented, her attorney could then come back and say, "But on the contrary, my client did not lie under oath; she simply stated, 'I do not recall.'" Look at the follow-up question that Kelli was asked while she was on the stand during the trial: "Is it possible you told him that?" (meaning could it have been possible that Kelli told Jerry that the detectives or the DA's office had instructed her not to talk to anyone who was helping Tonya?) Kelli had replied, "It could be"—again, another sidestep answer. No matter how you look at it, just based on her short testimony in which I was the topic of the questioning, Kelli McDonald was vague, unconvincing, and evasive—while under oath and in the presence of God. Yes, under God! Isn't that why we put our hand on the Bible during the swearing-in process?

Let's go back to Kelli telling her friend Sandra that her husband Jerry had talked to Tonya's private investigator. By now you have a fairly good picture of Sandra Lamb from the warts-and-all self-portrait painted with her own ugly words that day out in the middle of the street when I tried to serve her with papers and she went off her nut. I still had that little work of insane performance art on tape, both audio and video, safely tucked away, back at The LPS Group office. If you don't remember, let me refresh your memory. Sandra was identified and proven to be abusive, violent, and controlling. These traits were on full display and well documented. Her almost complete lack of truthfulness was proved in the wildly different versions of events as seen in the video and compared to the police report Sandra filed against me afterwards. Usually, in cases that hinge on such a difference of opinion as this, a person involved is left with nothing after the fact to resort to in his own defense but claims of "But—but she's a LIAR!" to back up his version. You know, the old "he said/she said" thing. But in this case, I don't *need* to say that, because the evidence is so abundant that the viewer can make the judgment in his or her own heart. Everything Sandra Lamb said, *plus* everything she did, was clearly, damningly caught on tape for everyone to see. Comparing Sandra's police report to the video and transcription of the incident clearly reveals Sandra as a person who does not tell the truth. Topping it off was her baffling willingness to give into blind rage and racial slurs even while she knew her actions and words were being preserved to be replayed again and again. It was as if the hostile face-smack she threw at me and the spat-out epithet—"You black bastard!"—were just business as usual for a woman who tried to present herself as a pillar of the community. At that moment when she claimed this big, terrifying, intimidating black man was absolutely scaring the pants off of her, Sandra Lamb was actually displaying no fear. It was as if she knew whatever was transpiring was going to be molded into the reality she wished. However that incident was going to play out during the trial, Sandra Lamb was far from done with me.

Now that your memory has been refreshed, who do you think Sandra called after being told that Jerry had talked to me? During her bizarre display, Sandra Lamb had bragged about her high-and-mighty local connections—so she got on the horn and dialed her good friend Chris Arnt, the chief district attorney for Catoosa County, and worked her magic. Whatever spin she put on her version of this incident is unknown—but considering her near-total varnishing of the facts in the false police report she had filed on me before, it's anybody's guess. The upshot is that Chris Arnt heard about my conversation with Jerry McDonald from the chattering mouth of Sandra Lamb, who as we have vividly seen is known to play fast and loose with the facts when it serves whatever personal end she has in mind. After he hung up the phone with Sandra, Chief District Attorney Arnt put into motion events that would change my life.

To understand the twists and turns of my story which shall follow, it's best if you know a little bit about the players we're about to meet. Fortunately, I know a lot about them, because I conducted investigations on each of them while I was on the case. So I'm going to introduce you to Chief District Attorney Chris Arnt, Detective Timothy Deal, and Detective Stephen Keith.

Before I turn to the results of the investigations I conducted on each of these men, let me say something that bears to be kept in mind here: People who work for the government, because of their positions, are to be held to a certain standard. These are people, who have been entrusted to be the moral conscience of our society, and as such, the life of a public servant is an open book—or, should I say, in the public record. The personal life of a government employee, especially one who occupies a high office or who has sworn an oath to protect the people, is subject to the public's scrutiny. Individuals who have been voted into office by the people of the county, city, state, or nation are compelled to perform their duties in as transparent a way as possible in full, open view of their constituents. And all elected public servants fall under this scrutiny, all the way up to the highest government position in the nation, the president of the United States. Judges, prosecutors, city officials, and the police are there to protect the public at large, defend the rights of all, and arrest and rightfully convict those who break the law. They have a sacred trust that goes along with all the privileges of power. In the offices they hold, they are expected to adhere to the letter of the law, to follow the spirit of the law in their quests to protect those who follow the law and those whom the law governs. It goes without saying that the people who are entrusted with such power are *not* there to make up laws as they see fit; nor should the law be twisted to suit their personal biases or serve their arrogance, ego or pride. The laws exist by general consent of we, the people—and no man or woman is above the law ... especially those who have been blessed enough to be in a position to defend the law.

That having been said, let's look first at the lead detective in the Tonya Craft case, Detective Tim Deal.

# DETECTIVE TIM DEAL — CATOOSA COUNTY SHERIFF

Detective Timothy Deal is a true native of small-town formalities. Deal was raised and has always lived in the town of Rossville in Walker County, Georgia—the county adjacent to Catoosa. When Deal was a little kid, all skinned knees and bright eyes full of promise, he was growing up in a place whose promise had died a few decades before. Rossville's decline was slow, ongoing, and never-ending, one of those tiny towns trying desperately to cling to its past as it was dissolving away. Rossville had once been a thriving cotton-mill town, but by the '60s when its main industries shut down or moved away, the local economy tanked and never fully recovered. By the time Deal graduated from Rossville High School in 1983, there wasn't much opportunity left in the way of decent jobs. When a whole block of downtown Rossville went up in flames in '87, that drove another stake into its financial heart. The commercial center of town eroded, and the long-time family-owned stores winked out, replaced by pawn shops and thrift stores.

Yet, somehow, Rossville still abides. Lying practically in the shadow of Chattanooga, Tennessee, Rossville sits to the south and just over the state line from one source of its ruin. Anyone who happens to wind up in Rossville is immediately drawn away by the magnetic pull of Chattanooga, and those who are left to struggle along, with a full 20 percent of Rossville's citizens scraping by below the poverty line. The population remaining is hardly what you could call a homogenous racial mix: it is currently over 93 percent white and under 4 percent black, with other minorities measured in handfuls—which, historically, is not how Rossville started out two hundred years ago.

Rossville gets its name from Chief John Ross, a chief of the Cherokee people who were the original residents of the area. Chief John Ross's father had been a white trader, the mixed blood giving the chief a compelling "in" with the white power structure; and with skill and diplomacy, Chief John Ross straddled the two differing cultures. But under President Andrew Jackson's Indian Removal "project," old alliances Jackson had made with the Cherokee and other tribes were disregarded. The Native nations he had exploited for the good of the new republic meant nothing when it came to Big Business as usual. So, because he was in the way of the sparkling American Dream of Manifest Destiny, the great Chief John Ross was kicked off his land—and then the US government kicked that poor betrayed man across half a continent along the Trail of Tears. Today, without a trace of irony, Chief John Ross's log cabin home is pimped as a local municipal historical treasure/tourist trap—and the proportion of Rossville's population that is Native American is just half of 1 percent.

So Rossville, Georgia, wouldn't exactly come to mind when you think of humanitarian awards. While I'm being a bit glib here, this is not a chip-on-my-shoulder issue about race—but I do want to give you an idea of the position I was in and the animosities I was about to face.

Now, I'm not naïve—I knew that there were pockets of provincial, backward thinking out there in the world, but anymore those places seemed to exist only in those old '70s drive-in movies. Frankly, I had gotten so used to the progressive mindset of the Atlanta area that I had begun to regard it as the norm—I mean, *hey!* We're in the *twenty-first century!* Having a few million people living in such close proximity to each other has helped a lot of the foolish old bigotries wither on the vine and die out. I'm not saying that it's not a big interracial peace-and-love hugfest here; even in a city as cosmopolitan as Atlanta, race is still a hot-button issue at times. But for the most part, people are just getting used to seeing each other as *people*. Things were chill on a scale that had given me the grace to relax. In my life, there wasn't that background level of prejudice that my parents and grandparents had had to endure, the social separation, the constant, lonely sense of being regarded as a sort of Frankenstein monster in the room. If anything, the new line in the sand between human beings was not one of race but one of class, of status; and I had achieved that. I had worked hard, stayed determined, led an upright life, and made a success of myself. It was a new century, and it was wonderful to be living in the future, where I was first and foremost accepted and respected as a *man*.

But even something so basic as a man's sense of self-respect can be warped by outside forces. Just taking an afternoon's drive north of this urban mecca of enlightened racial equality showed me that the years of advancements were suddenly gone with the wind. The more I was pulled north to my business in Catoosa County and the surrounding territory, the more I noticed the difference. Sometimes as I headed up I-75, I could see time peeling away in my movie-nut's mind as the calendar pages blew past me with every mile—June, May, April, March—back into the '80s, the '70s, the '60s ... all the way from civil rights to uncivil wrongs. How far back into the past could it go?

I can honestly say the Craft case was not about race, but considering the mindset I was up against in that corner of the state, the entirely incidental fact of my race couldn't help play a role in the whole thing—often in ways I never expected.

Now back to Detective Deal. I had amassed a history of Deal's education and his professional career, and I clicked through the details. Deal had gone to Covenant College in Lookout Mountain, Georgia, and Dalton College in Dalton, Georgia, just a stone's throw from Catoosa County. He then attended the University of Tennessee at Chattanooga.

His next career path had given me the momentary expectation that he might be a compassionate guy, but I had to accept the fact that sometimes a general rule just wouldn't fit for every subject. Like Jerry McDonald, Deal also was certified as a paramedic and a CPR/First Aid Instructor. At one point, Deal worked for Hutcheson Medical Center and Whitfield Emergency Medical Services. I wondered if Deal had worked for Dwayne Wilson during this time. You see, Dwayne Wilson owned Angel Emergency Medical Service, and this region was a comparatively small pond for these various emergency services to be working. Jurisdictions overlapped and multiple units often made the same call, giving me the idea that Wilson and Deal could possibly know each other. In their professional capacities, the chances were better than good that their paths crossed often enough, because Wilson is also the county coroner—as well as being the angry, red-faced parent who had threatened Tonya Craft that he would "get" her for not passing his daughter to the next grade, bellowing that she was "not going to embarrass [his] family." This was beginning to get complicated—here were a pivotal player in the Craft case and the DA on the case possibly rubbing elbows professionally. This tangled net of connections and intertwined lives was beginning to get snarled. But the possibility of a prior connection between

Dwayne Wilson and Detective Deal only added fuel to my investigation.

Detective Deal had worked for a few police departments before ending up as a Catoosa County Sheriff. These small-town Georgia police departments include: Tunnel Hill Police Department, Dalton City Police Department, and Fort Oglethorpe Police Department... Just picture the size of the police department in the TV show "In the Heat of the Night," and there you are. After discovering some employment history on Deal, I first wanted to find out what officer training he had received during his career. I also wanted to find out the specifics of the training and the total amount of training— especially how much of Deal's forensic police training was associated with the particular crimes with which Tonya was charged. This is what I found:

Detective Deal conducted one thousand eight hundred and forty (1,840) training hours from October 15, 1984, to February 20, 2009. This factors out to be seventy-three-point-six (73.6) hours of training a year.

During this time, Detective Deal has had the following training dealing with children and juveniles:

1. 8/31/2001        Child Abuse Investigators Course
        40 hours
2. 10/10/2001      Crimes Against Children
        8 hours
3. 12/11/2003      Missing Children
        2 hours
4. 8/9/2007        Child Pornography Investigations
        8 hours

There were only fifty-eight documented training hours relating to crimes against children and only eight documented training hours relating to the charges of which Tonya was accused. This is less than half a percent (.43%) of Detective Deal's total training in the twenty-six years since he became a police officer and a paramedic.

I prefaced this part of the book earlier by mentioning that public servants must face a certain measure of transparency for the benefit and reassurance of the people. Fortunately, there is legislation in place that ensures this: the Open Records Act, or ORA, is an invaluable source of public information about our officials. That was what I used for conducting the initial phase of my investigation into this subject's background. ORA requests got me all of Detective Deal's employment files from each police department where he was employed during his career as an police officer. I also got invaluable contact info, so I was able to call and talk to Detective Deal's prior supervisors. The conversation that proved most fruitful for my investigation was the conversation I had with Chief Brunson of the Tunnel Hill Police Department. His insights helped draw a visual graph between the level of a fully trained professional and that of Detective Deal. During our conversation, I asked Chief Brunson how many training hours a lead detective should have if he or she were assigned to handling child molestation cases. Chief Brunson stated that a lead detective handling child molestation cases should have at least a couple of hundred hours of training in that specific area. The records showed that Deal only had fifty-eight (58) hours, a quarter of the minimum requirement. Further on in our conversation, I asked Chief Brunson, "Should an officer be a lead detective if he has less than a hundred hours of POST training?" (POST stands for Peace

Officer Standards and Training, an important component in the overall proficiency measurement of an officer.) Chief Brunson thought about this, and then retraced his steps a bit. He stated that he should not have said a couple of hundred hours, and he added that the person in question could have worked under a lead detective on other child molestation cases in the field, receiving hours of real-world experience. Chief Brunson went on to say that such experience hours would not show in the officer's POST training. This information seemed valid and sensible. To verify this theory, I used the Open Records Act and sent requests to all the police departments where Detective Deal had been employed, including Catoosa County.

The ORA request that I sent to the police departments of Tunnel Hill, Dalton, Fort Oglethorpe, and the Catoosa County Sheriff's office is as follows.

Dear Custodian of Records:

I wanted to send you an open records request pursuant to O.C.G.A. §50-18-70 for the total number of cases, the case number(s), and disposition of Child Molestation cases and Aggravated Sexual Battery cases involving minors and children whereas Detective Timothy D. Deal, was the Lead Officer investigating the case, or a documented supporting Officer investigating on the case.

As you are aware, the City has three (3) business days to respond to this request. Obviously, if there are any charges for the gathering of the documents relevant to this request, I will gladly pay the same.
Thank you for your prompt attention to this matter and I look forward to hearing from you soon.

Very truly yours,

Eric D. Echols, CFI
The LPS Group, Inc.

When returned, the replies to the ORA requests revealed the following:

1.  Tunnel Hill Police – Treasa West, City Clerk, Tunnel Hill, stated that Detective Deal never was a lead investigator on aggravated sexual battery cases or child molestation investigations. West stated that Tunnel Hill is a small department and does not employ any detectives. All investigative work would have been turned over to Whitfield County (*from e-mail received from West on Wednesday March 18, 2009*).

2.  Dalton Police Department – Trocye S. Nash replied that cases involving minors and children from November 16, 1987, to December 15, 1991, in which Detective Timothy D. Deal was the officer investigating, included one case documents: case number #90-006017, which was unfounded (*response letter received from Mr. Nash on March 17, 2009*).

3.  Fort Oglethorpe Police Department – Ronald C. Goulart, City Manager, stated, "Please be advised that we do not have any records that indicate that Detective Timothy D. Deal investigated any of the cases alluded to in your letter. Our records indicate that Detective Timothy Deal was employed by our City as a part-time dispatcher and police officer."

4.  Catoosa County Sheriff – Someone in the sheriff's office who did not sign the document replied to the request by sending case numbers typed on a sheet of paper with "45 TOTAL CASES: Child molestation and/or aggravated sexual battery cases from June 14, 2006, to present" (*"present" being at the time March 2009*). NOTE: Out of those forty-five cases sent by Catoosa County per the ORA, only two cases were

incidents involving adult female offenders and juvenile female victims, and one of the cases was identified as Tonya Henke Craft's.

The comments that Detective Deal's supervisors had made in his personnel file described Deal as being a good police officer. However, the small towns where he had worked scarcely offered an environment that would seriously test a detective's mettle. I couldn't help but think of the jumpy Deputy Barney Fife with his empty gun and his single bullet in his uniform pocket. Still, that was a wrong image—the world was ugly, and no police officer anywhere exactly had it easy. But the overriding point was that there just wasn't that much hands-on crime to study, and Detective Deal's police background clearly illustrated that he lacked the professional POST-certified training and police field casework experience to be a lead detective on a high-profile child molestation case such as the Tonya Craft case. This conclusion was solely based on the results gathered during the course of my investigation.

In Georgia, as in any other state, when city and county police departments are faced with a high-profile case that requires a superior amount of experience in pursuing and prosecuting the particular crime that has been alleged, they can seek assistance from another branch of state or federal law enforcement. The Catoosa County sheriff should have exercised this request. Now, the question could be posed that if the Catoosa County Sheriff's Office had indeed been willing to request expert assistance in prosecuting child molestation cases, as was certainly within its right, how could that have affected Tonya's case? My answer would be— in my professional opinion—that the experts would then have fully, thoroughly investigated the case and would have conducted proper interviews with the alleged victims, and most importantly of all: these outside experts would not have made this case personal. The end result could have been Tonya's exoneration—if she were even charged at all.

## DETECTIVE STEPHEN KEITH — CATOOSA COUNTY SHERIFF

The investigation into Detective Stephen B. Keith started out much the same way that Deal's had: the names of places varied, but Stephen Keith's life story was another version of the small-town background and its attendant limitations. Even the general locale was the same—Walker County, nestled next to Catoosa, up in that hilly northwest corner of Georgia. Keith went to LaFayette High School in LaFayette, Georgia, from 1984 to 1988. In the fall of 1989, Keith attended Dalton College; however, he never completed his studies there, instead dropping out of college. Starting while he was still attending Dalton College, Keith burned through a series of low-paying jobs: he worked for the Chrysler dealership in Ringgold from August 1988 to September 1989 and then moved on to Perry's Seafood restaurant in Chattanooga, Tennessee from September 1898 to March 1990; a factory job at Synthetic Industries in Chickamauga, Georgia March 1990 to September 1990. Then he went back to Ringgold to work at Salem Carpets from November 1990 to January 1991. So what does this all mean? Well, it's not exactly the résumé of someone who applies himself to education or earning a living: after Keith got out of high school and ditched college, from September 1989 to January 1991, he worked for four different places of employment—four jobs in sixteen months' time. Furthermore, the record showed that he had been terminated from Synthetic Industries. His reasoning behind why he was fired was that he had missed three work days during his probationary period. Two of the days he had missed, Keith claimed, were due to his wife having given birth to a baby.

Now, I admit that I do not know about the policies regarding maternity leave where you work, but when one of my employees has a wife who is having a baby, we give the husband time off and send the couple a gift card. The reason Keith cited for why he was terminated did not seem to be truthful. Knowing the south as being "The Bible Belt," I'm sure that allowing a new father at least two days off is an excusable reason and the days off would not count against the employee. I wondered if that had truly been the real reason, or if the real reason Keith was absent had actually been something much more damaging. For example, did Synthetic Industries have a drug-testing policy, and if so, did Keith fail a drug test? According to something I found later in his timeline, there was a distinct possibility of that.

The notes in Keith's file trace that path all the way back to December of 1989. A document sworn and attested to by a Lieutenant Morrison noted that Keith smoked marijuana at a New Year's Eve party. This would have been right before Keith worked with Synthetic Industries—and right before he applied with the Catoosa County Sheriff's Department to be a detention officer. Along with Lt. Morrison's report, it was also noted in Keith's file that he had had a few infractions with the law. Within eight months, Keith racked up three speeding tickets: in June 1989, he was stopped in Ringgold, Georgia; in February 1990, a cop pulled him over in Summerville, Georgia,; and in March 1990, he was caught lead-footing it through Rock Spring, Georgia. I do not know the state, city, or county where this is not considered a blatant disregard of the law. This strange portrait of our detective subject was shaping up to be something you'd find in a rogue's gallery.

Here is what I was thinking: Keith moved around from job to job, he was witnessed smoking an illegal substance, and he was a noted traffic offender and scofflaw. These incidents all occurred not long before Keith applied to the Catoosa County Sheriff's Department in January of 1991. Many would question whether Keith, after having been caught engaging in this documented unlawful behavior, should ever have been hired as a Catoosa County sheriff's deputy. But, miraculously, he was.

Further investigation into Detective Keith's law-enforcement history revealed more of his contempt for the rules. Within a year after he was hired by Catoosa County Sheriff's Department, Keith was on the receiving end of a series of disciplinary actions. The infractions started on August 12, 1991, with a failure to report to a mandatory detention meeting; then on January 17, 1992, for failure to report to an assigned shift on that day; and again on March 2, 1992, for failure to report for assigned shifts. To show how undisciplined the young cadet was, on February 22, Keith showed up for duty one hour and fifty-three minutes late, and he upped his score a week later, when, without reporting to the supervisor, he dragged in to work one hour and fifty-eight minutes late. Taken as a script for a goofy *Police Academy* movie, this scenario has comedy possibilities—but come on, this is the real world. Even though the Catoosa County beat was a mostly uneventful detail to pull, he was still a cop, a police officer, a man with a badge who took an oath of commitment to duty. But if Keith was even aware he was supposed to uphold a standard, he seemed to treat the whole thing as a joke. These repeated occurrences implied not only a lack of respect for authority, but they painted a picture of someone who didn't possess the responsible character necessary to be an officer of the law. These disciplinary actions were confirmation of that assessment. One would think that after these failures, Keith would have been terminated. But he was not.

As I delved deeper into Detective Keith's bizarre law-enforcement career with the Catoosa County Sheriff's Department, what I found further demonstrated the veracity of my assessment during the background investigation. His career, to be kind, went all over the damned place. Keith had served in the Detention Unit until October 5, 1992, when he signed the Oath of Deputy Sheriff and rose in the ranks—and then three years later, on October 9, 1995, out of the blue, Deputy Keith resigned his position with the department. After that, a quick half a year rolls past, and by April 29, 1996, Keith was rehired by the Catoosa County Sheriff's Department as a patrolman.

I rubbed my eyes and looked again at the dates. Did that place have a revolving-door policy? In October, he's out—then a quick half a year rolls past, and by April, he's back in their good graces. This six-month break raised several questions. Why did Keith resign, only to return to the Catoosa County Sheriff's Department after six months? Was the "temporary" resignation due to personal issues? Was it due to drug issues? Was it due to quitting before he could get terminated over some infraction? What made him realize that he stood a chance of getting back in?

These are questions that will require further investigations. I will say that when Keith went back to work, he came in as a patrolman and worked his way up to the position of lieutenant – shift supervisor. Then on April 23, 2004, Lt. Keith requested a self-demotion to patrol deputy, citing family obligations as a compelling reason. During this time, Keith and his ex-wife were locked in a child-custody battle; at this time, Keith became the school resource officer at Lakeview – Ft. Oglethorpe High School.

Even after fourteen years with the Catoosa County Sheriff's Department , Keith continued his disregard for authority. On April 26, 2005, Deputy Keith was lawfully subpoenaed to appear in probate court but failed to appear (*memo in file dated May 3, 2005*). After all this, on November 2, 2006, Deputy Keith was transferred to the Detective Division of the Catoosa County Sheriff's Department.

Let me sum this man's baffling résumé up: The investigation of Detective Keith's background prior to his becoming an employee of the Catoosa County Sheriff's Department, and then throughout his ensuing career as a deputy with Catoosa County, revealed the paper trail of a person who consistently displayed a lack of respect for authority, paid no attention to rules, broke the law, and exhibited questionable actions that impugned his character and integrity as an officer of the law. And yet, despite all this seemingly damning evidence, Keith has somehow managed to avoid punishment for his actions and has, on the contrary, moved up through the system to become a full-fledged detective.

Now that I had a grip on Detective Keith's checkered background—where he went to school, his work history, plus his police career and his performance as a police officer—it was time to find out what training Keith had received as a police officer. More specifically, I wanted to know the extent of his training in the areas relating to the crimes with which Tonya was charged. Here is what I found:

Detective Keith conducted nine hundred and fifty-three (953) training hours from May 28, 1991, through August 28, 2008. During this time, Detective Keith had the following training dealing with children and juveniles:

1. 08/19/1999 Juvenile Counseling
   4 hours
2. 03/20/2008 Child Injury & Death Investigations
   12 hours

I looked through it to make sure all the figures were there, but that was it—the sum total of the specialized documented training dealing with children or juveniles that this officer of the law had received in almost two decades was only sixteen hours! Furthermore, there was *no* documented training relating specifically to the charges of which Tonya was accused. The amount of training Detective Keith had with issues related to children was only 1.7 percent of his total training in the seventeen years since he had become a detention officer and deputy sheriff. Just as when I was investigating Detective Deal, I used the Open Records Act and requested all child molestation and/or aggravated sexual battery cases in which Detective Keith was the lead detective, documented supporting detective, or officer investigating the case. I only had to send the ORA to the Catoosa County Sheriff's Department, as this is the only police department where Keith had been employed. The response from Catoosa County specified that Detective Keith had investigated twenty-three (23) total cases involving child molestation and/or aggravated sexual battery from April 29, 1996, to the present (*March 2009*).

All of Detective Keith's cases that were identified by Catoosa County Sheriff per the ORA were dated November 2007 to February 2009. This means that Keith had only worked investigating child molestation and/or aggravated sexual battery cases for just over one year prior to the Tonya Craft case. Also, Detective Keith had no prior field experience with these types of cases. Of the twenty-three cases, *none* involved female offenders and juvenile female victims. During that time, the only case that Detective Keith was assigned to and worked on in which there was an alleged female offender and juvenile female victims was the Tonya Henke Craft case.

My investigation of Detective Stephen Keith had proved to be a real head-shaker because it vividly showed that Keith clearly did not have the training to even be an assisting detective on the Tonya Craft case. Further, Keith lacked the professional POST-certified training and had no prior police field casework experience. In fact, based on the woefully low numbers and the disturbing details about his personal life and criminal record that I had uncovered, my investigation showed that Detective Keith probably should not have even been employed with the Catoosa County Sheriff's Department, at least not in 1991.

Having Deal and Keith as the acting detectives on the Tonya Craft case was an invitation to inferior investigations, mediocre case development, and appallingly unprofessional police behavior. Any law-enforcement professionals coming up against something big and crucial would have requested partnering with an outside agency or getting assistance from another state or federal agency. That possibility was becoming common knowledge in our day and age. I mean, don't they watch *Criminal Minds* in Catoosa County? Why was the concept of requesting assistance from someone with more experience not an option in the Tonya Craft case? Why wouldn't they open up their investigation to someone from the outside? That just didn't make sense.

Unless...

Unless there was something the Catoosa County authorities did not want to leave Catoosa County.

# CHRISTOPHER A. ARNT – CHIEF ASSISTANT DISTRICT ATTORNEY

The investigation I conducted into the background of Christopher A. Arnt, chief assistant district attorney, Lookout Mountain Judicial Circuit, Catoosa County, was very enlightening. So let's begin...

Christopher Allen Anthony Arnt graduated in 1984 from McIntosh High School in Peachtree City, Georgia, and proceeded to Tulane University in New Orleans, Louisiana, until 1989. After that, he did a turn at Emory University School of Law in Atlanta, Georgia. Arnt met and married Tracy Lynn Kozimor; subsequently, the Arnts had two children. Right out of Emory University School of Law, Arnt was hired by Judge Ralph Van Pelt, who was the district attorney for Catoosa County in the Lookout Mountain Judicial Circuit from 1989 to 1996. Van Pelt tapped Arnt to be an assistant district attorney, and during his eighteen years within the District Attorney's Office, Arnt had a pretty good career. He proved to be an ambitious go-getter and worked his way up the ranks to chief district attorney for the Lookout Mountain Judicial Circuit District Attorney's Office in 2009. In his tenure as Catoosa County DA, Chris Arnt has prosecuted and won several cases involving child molestation, child pornography, infant death, murder, sex crimes, and the list goes on. Arnt was even on the team investigating the nationally known Tri-State Crematory scandal, the grisly and baffling case in which hundreds of bodies, officially turned over to Tri-State for cremation, had actually been stacked up like cordwood and hidden, for reasons unknown, by the crematory operator. In his career, Arnt has been recognized by his peers: he was identified in *Super Lawyers* magazine as a "Super Lawyer" in 2007, and in 2008, Arnt received the J. Roger Thompson Award for actively teaching young prosecutors, a task which he has been doing for the past fourteen years (at the time of writing this book). The presenter of the award even stated that Arnt "*...is a prosecutor dedicated to fairness, and has a strong adherence to professionalism, ethics, and moral obligation.*" Arnt was a lecturer, active in his church, a soccer referee for kids, and a member of the Knights of Columbus. What I found in my initial research into the background of Chris Arnt indicated that he was all about justice and fair treatment. I located Arnt's signed oath that he took when he was hired by the State of Georgia for Lookout Mountain Judicial Circuit. Here is what it states:

### OATH OF ASSISTANT DISTRICT ATTORNEY
### STATE OF GEORGIA
### LOOKOUT MOUNTAIN JUDICAL CIRCUIT

I, Christopher A. Arnt, do swear that I will faithfully and impartially, and without fear, favor or affection, discharge my duties as Assistant District Attorney, and will take only my lawful compensation.

I do further solemnly swear and affirm that I am not the holder of any unaccounted public money due this state; that I am not the holder of any office of trust under the government of the United States, nor of any foreign state; and, that I am otherwise qualified to hold said office, according to the Constitution and Laws of Georgia, and that I will support the Constitution of the United States and of this State.

SO HELP ME GOD!

[*signed*]
Christopher A. Arnt
ASSISTANT DISTRICT ATTORNEY
LOOKOUT MOUNTAIN JUDICAL CIRCUIT

Sworn to and subscribed before me this 17th day of August, 1992.

[*signed*]
Foye L. Johnson
Probate Judge


As I read the oath that Arnt swore, attested to, and signed when he was hired in 1992, I could only wonder what had happened to Chris Arnt and that high-sounding vow he had taken back then. Because the man at the beginning of the glowing profile didn't match the one I was familiar with at the other end of the timeline. Something had happened to change that straight and narrow course Arnt had started out on. Maybe I could figure out what it was.

Something that gives all aspects of my career and my life a particular edge is the fact that I'm a fairly good reader of human nature. I've been around the block more than most people, but I didn't let it get me dizzy—on my trip through this life, I've kept alert and watched, observed, and learned. Maybe this change in Arnt was a case of that age-old human complaint: the monster inside.

I guess everyone must have one monster in there (some people seem to have even more!), but it's a measure of our self-discipline to keep those base impulses in check, to rise above them and become better people. Some people are wrestling with their natures more than you can tell, and when that other side of them comes out, BOOM. For better or for worse, it can be explosive. As a US Marine, I've seen men I thought were weak as wet straw suddenly, in the heat of a crisis, show that they're made out of steel cable and adrenaline. And that is thrilling to witness. But other times in my life, I've seen it go the other way. When the wrong perspectives are fed, it seems like the firmest convictions can crumble like clay. It's a disappointing fact of human nature. People start out with the purest of intentions—and then it's like something just turns around inside their hearts, like a one-eighty that rips all the wiring out and makes them act totally unlike the person you used to know. They get a taste of something that they like more than anything else and they're *gone*. Sometimes the catalyst that tips them over is drugs. Sometimes it's love, like dangerous, bad love. And sometimes, it's something as false and insubstantial as a feeling of power.

But that'll do it. Even on a penny-ante level, a decade and a half of wielding power can be enough to change a personality, bending it at its weak spots and warping it from civic-minded superego into self-inflating ego mixed with unchecked, rampaging id. It's a change that can sneak up even on some naive do-gooder type. As he goes along there in the focal point of the fishbowl, he starts to feel an emotional hunger awaken, a need for attention, for that warm, warm spotlight. The desire to serve becomes entwined with the desire to be *seen* serving—and delusion follows: An unattractively blocky red-brick "justice building" becomes a stately, classical Greek-style courthouse; the sparse main street of a rural hamlet becomes a New York grand avenue; and the hole-in-the-wall restaurant down the street becomes an extension of that same sweet stage.

In the beginning, he used to stroll to lunch. Now the short walk is a one-man parade. When he swaggers in and cruises to his favorite corner table in the little place, a handful of local heads turn in his direction and that ego-fire is stroked. When he speaks, he speaks so bystanders can hear; when he laughs, he laughs too loudly. Even on his own time, he "holds court"—pointed pun intended. The waitresses fawn and flirt, and the hot flush of authority makes his chest swell like he can bench press 300lbs. Glad-handers in outdated suits approach to curry his favor, slap his back, and kiss his ass—and the hungry little thing inside him feeds deep...

I considered my scenario and wondered. *Was this the cause of the change in him?* I had to ask myself. Because it seemed from the evidence I found that there was a *before* and *after* here that didn't quite match. This perception may sound biased, but believe me when I say that this is solely based on the overall investigation in the Craft case and my eyewitness accounts of Arnt's unprofessional behavior in the courtroom during the motion hearings I attended. The first sentence of that oath that Arnt signed states: *"I will faithfully and impartially, and without fear, favor or affection, discharge my duties as Assistant District Attorney, and will take only my lawful compensation."* Based on not only what you have read here, but also what you can follow on the Internet, in the television news archives and on the blogs, the evidence showed that the straight arrow was veering off the course he had sworn to follow. Arnt was not honoring his oath.

Lest you think this is just my opinion, which could be from a perspective slanted by what I endured thanks to the machinations of this man, there were other people avidly following every in and out of this case as it transpired, and they came away from the Tonya Craft trial with the same point of view. Those who are interested can read for themselves the running account of one of those concerned citizens. William L. Anderson, an economics professor at Frostburg State University in Maryland, maintains a blog. He became intrigued by the bizarre nature of the Tonya Craft case, also noticing as many others had that things were just not adding up. He began reporting on developments regarding the case and my arrest and provided a straightforward, factual account of wrongdoings by Judge House, District Attorneys Chris Arnt and Len Gregor, Detective Deal, and the prosecution witnesses. It has been clearly shown that Arnt's thought process could hardly be called impartial. Since it was not a part of my investigation, I won't enumerate all the court proceedings in which Arnt, Gregor, or even Judge House displayed a lack of ethics and professionalism while in the courtroom. However, the phase "without favor" is something I can talk about in regard to the case. If a "good friend"—which is how Sandra Lamb referred to Arnt in that formal police report—calls you up and claims, "Tonya Craft molested my daughter and these other little girls," then, being a good friend, Arnt apparently naturally did everything in his power to prosecute and secure a conviction against Tonya Craft—just because his good friend Sandra told him that this woman she disliked had messed with her daughter and other little girls. However, I needed to prove that this was Arnt's motive. I needed hard evidence that Chief District Attorney Chris Arnt was somehow doing a favor for Sandra because of their being "good friends"—or out of some deeper affection Arnt had toward Sandra that was built in the course of their friendship.

Sometimes a big fish in a small pond can lose all perspective about his true stature and just how tiny his realm of influence really is. Even in a little jerkwater town like Ringgold, Georgia, occupying a high government position is enough to give an egotistical person an inflated sense of self-importance. My grandmother, may she rest in peace, used to call it "smelling yourself," or "acting like your shit don't stink"—an earthy but on-target illustration of a person with a pompous, pretentious attitude. Throughout my investigation I noted it, and in the courtroom most of the people there seemed to notice, too, how Arnt displayed this type of attitude, but the question was why? Why was Arnt behaving in this manner? Was it because he had been recognized with awards? Was it because he was more than good friends with Sandra? Was it because Sandra came from money, and Arnt wanted some sort of connection to that influence? Or was it because Arnt wanted Sandra's or the Lamb family's support while running for Superior Court Judge in the Lookout Mountain Judicial District during this time? Just so you know: Arnt was up against a formidable field of rivals in this race. The four other candidates for the vacant judge's seat were Mike Giglio, Brian House (who won), Bill Rhyne Jr., and Larry Stagg, who was Sandra Lamb's attorney. *Hmm,* I thought, *another Sandra connection*—but in this case, Stagg was on the other side there, running against Arnt. Everything was so interconnected in this little place that it seemed like some incestuous *HeeHaw* joke.

One of my favorite movies is *Contact*, starring Jodie Foster. In the movie, Foster plays a scientist who is convinced there is life on other planets. Her scientist colleagues receive her ideas with skepticism and ridicule, but through her tenacity she proves that there indeed *is* life somewhere besides here on earth. There was a scene in the movie when Foster's character, Dr. Arroway, is asked if she is familiar with the concept of Occam's razor; she replies something along the lines of "It's the principle that the simplest explanation is usually the correct one." Well, applying this principle to Arnt, on one level it could just mean that Arnt has a strong arrogant streak. That's certainly not an actionable offense, or else the prisons would be even more full to bursting; as I've had to explain to some of my clients before, as unfortunate as it is, there is no criminal statute to prevent someone from acting like an asshole. But personality conflicts aside, something about the connections that seemed to be spiderwebbing all over the place made me consider that there could be strings attached to the other players through Arnt. I knew damn well where one of those strings led—because that relationship had been literally rubbed in my face by Sandra Lamb. And being an investigator, my role was to investigate the relationship and determine the ties between Arnt and Sandra Lamb. As I stated earlier, we had kept Sandra under mobile surveillance, which had not at the time revealed any fraternization with Arnt, Joal Henke, or Detective Deal.

Politicians are known for veering from the true path at times. A man can enter elected office with the purest of intentions; but then, to some men, that seat of power begins to feel more and more like a throne. When the man in that seat is weak-willed or when it comes to resisting the pull of his own ego, that's a formula for corruption. That's when the office becomes a personal convenience, and the law goes out the window along with the best interests of the people. Money, power, sex, and ambition are powerful lures for more than their immediate qualities; they can also serve to fill the empty gulfs in a damaged personality. Making decisions based on money, power, sex and ambition has ruined many of political careers, families, and friendships, especially if the way they were obtained was through unethical means or with malice. An example of this was my arrest for interviewing Jerry McDonald. It is difficult to see my arrest as anything other than a direct and explicit example of Arnt using unethical means to favor his good friend Sandra Lamb. To violate the civil rights of a person, no matter what the reason is a slap in the face of lady justice and our constitution. This act without a doubt served to send the message to Sandra that her good pal Arnt supported her and had her back. There was something going on there that made her fearless in the face of contradictory, provable evidence. Remember the false statement Sandra made to the police when I was trying to conduct that court-ordered process service. She again made a false statement in a police report involving me—the one that was presented to the Grand Jury to secure my arrest for the three felony counts of witness influencing.

So the question remains, why was Arnt so connected to Sandra? Why was he willing to do whatever she wanted him to do? A long time ago, when I first started doing investigations, the rule of thumb I followed was to follow the money. This concept of "follow the money" has been the fact findings behind many investigations. If someone was stealing or perpetrating fraud, the common goal was to get money. And Sandra Lamb, from all reports, was all about money and influence. Did Sandra give money to Arnt to secure his involvement in prosecuting Tonya— or, perhaps, even in the pursuit of having me arrested? On my indictment, Sandra Lamb's name was listed as a witness, though I did not interview her. One thing I knew for sure was that Sandra Lamb came from money and had money—and when that was weighed against the fact that her good friend Chris Arnt was ambitiously eyeing a judge's seat, it gave rise to the possibility that there was something tangible there. Using the "follow the money" theory, I began to look at how Sandra could have given Arnt money. This is what was found.

When running for government office in Georgia, each individual who receives contributions above a certain amount must itemize contributions on the State of Georgia Campaign Contribution Disclosure Report. This rule requires all candidates to list all monies received from each single contributor for whom the aggregate total is $101 or more. The report marked "Election Year December 31, 2008" that was e-filed on January 1, 2009, listed a fact that raised both my eyebrows when I saw it. There, in black and white, the report stated that on December 11, 2008, Larry Stagg of Ringgold, Georgia, made a donation to Christopher Arnt for two thousand dollars.

*What?* That was when things totally went through the looking glass here. The fact that Larry Stagg was Sandra's attorney raised a red flag—but what was even more baffling is that when Larry Stagg made this contribution to Arnt's campaign fund, at that time he was locked in a pitched political battle against Arnt for the very same judge's seat! Why was Larry Stagg unaccountably giving his opponent—two thousand bucks to fuel the campaign against him? *What the hell*, I thought, shaking my head. Two men, rivals for the same position—and here is cold, hard evidence that one guy is underwriting the other guy's political war machine. That's a detail that just jumps out at you.

While reviewing the reports, I also noticed something else. In my investigation on Arnt, it was discovered with his wife Tracy, Arnt is co-owner of Locomotion Promotions, a small company dealing in promotional products, based in Ringgold. I noticed in the records that Arnt was giving himself loans—which is fine, ordinarily, depending on where the money came from—using his own company, Locomotion Promotions. Here's where it wanders into an ethical grey area, he was using Locomotion Promotions for his campaign promotional items and then turning around and paying Locomotion from monies he received as campaign contributions. Now, I'm not a forensic accountant, but paying yourself from donations under your company name is questionable—especially in the case of a judicial expert. Arnt's financial records showed a loss during the campaign when he was running for judge, based on monies which he had noted on the Campaign Contribution Disclosure Report as being loans from himself and expenditures of Locomotion Promotions. On the report, marked "Election Year September 30, 2008," that was e-filed on October 1, 2008, Arnt reported that he himself had given his own campaign $23,200 on September 30, 2008. As I stated before, I'm not a forensic accountant, but as a private investigator I would like to know if these funds can be verified and justified. After all, Arnt is a government employee who was running for an elected position—and remember, persons occupying those positions must expect their moves to be an open book. Below are some other things I would like to know, if I were looking further into the campaign fund of Arnt:

1. Can Arnt show that $23,200 was taken out of his personal checking or savings account, and if so, does the account show consistent deposits to accumulate the amount of $23,200?

2. Did the $23,200 come from his business account, and if so, does the account show consistent deposits to accumulate the amount of $23,200?

3. Does the personal or business account show large deposits before the date of September 30, 2008, and if so, from whom did they come? Were they deposits of cash or checks? If they were checks, from what person or company were they drawn?

4. Do Arnt's business taxes filed for the year 2008 show a loss, and if so, is it stated on the forms that the reason for the loss was the failed campaign for the judge's seat for the Lookout Mountain Judicial Circuit? If so, what was the total amount of the claimed financial loss?

What emerged overall is some questionable activity, not the least of which is the baffling fact that Larry Stagg gave Arnt—his political rival who was running for the very same office he himself was—two thousand bucks for his campaign. I know $2,000 does not seem like that much money, but I'm sure we all know of cases in which people have done much worse for a lot less. Really, though, that's beside the point here: this is something that majorly just does not make a lick of sense. Look at it this way: it's a bit like if, during the 2008 presidential campaign, Sarah Palin gave Barack Obama a campaign donation, smiled and slapped him on the back, shook his hand, and wished him well. Even a high school student running for class president is not going to give a platter of cookies and brownies to the other candidates running against him/her and then just let them turn around pass out the goodies to the student body to win voters away.

Finally, Arnt using his own company for services during a campaign isn't questionable—it's downright unethical. The private investigators who work for The LPS Group, Inc., have all been trained by third-party licensed instructors with the Georgia Board of Private Detectives and Security Agencies. Why? Because even though I'm also a certified instructor with the Georgia Board of Private Detectives and Security Agencies, I do not want to leave any questionable thought in the mind of the Georgia Board Members. The eliminates any doubt that the training actually took place or the possibility for someone to question whether I just said it did to get my employees their private investigators' licenses. Did Chris Arnt actually use his company Locomotion Productions for campaign materials, or was that a way Arnt paid himself money from contributions? The actions of a person running for an elected position should be above reproach. Arnt was not. Of all the individuals we investigated and those individuals I interviewed, the actions in this case of Christopher A. Arnt, Chief District Attorney for Catoosa County, most significantly warrant further scrutiny on a higher level by other federal agencies. It is my belief and the belief of others that his actions in the Tonya Craft case demonstrate unethical and possibly criminal behavior.

I know there are some who will point the finger and say that I'm simply being vindictive, that I'm out for revenge. That would be a natural reaction, given the circumstances so far and as you read further along in this book, you'll see that I have abundant personal reasons to loathe this particular human being. Yes, it is true that I was wronged by the actions of this man. But, as we've found so far with each of the players in this high-stakes backwater soap opera, it's the person's own words and actions that do the job for me. The sweet thing is that I don't have to point the finger at Chris Arnt, because he pointed three fingers back at himself every time he theatrically stabbed his finger in the air in that courtroom. What he did and what he thought of me is largely a matter of public record. And I think it was damned thoughtful of him, hoisting himself high like that, where everyone could see.

# INVESTIGATING THE STATE AGENCIES AND THE PEOPLE BEHIND THEM

During the course of the Craft investigation, it slowly began to become apparent that both the prosecution and the witnesses for the prosecution had the same agenda, and it wasn't an agenda to find truth and justice. It seemed to be an agenda to "Get Tonya Craft and those working on her behalf"—with a subheading on it that read "Make sure Tonya doesn't see her daughter." To confirm this, I began investigating additional individuals and agencies that had any direct involvement with the Craft case. This also included those who had direct contact with the alleged victims from the beginning. This list included child therapist Laurie Evans, nurse Sharon Anderson (Sexual Assault Nurse Examiner – SANE), the Children's Advocacy Center for the Lookout Mountain Judicial Circuit, and Four Points, Inc., a nonprofit organization offering assistance to families dealing with domestic violence which was located in LaFayette, Georgia.

The investigative plan from this point on was to find out if the individuals who examined the alleged victims mentally and physically were actually capable of doing so. It also was meant to determine if all of the agencies' policies and procedures were in fact followed to the letter and not circumvented because of the prosecution's eagerness to convict Tonya Craft without a fair trial.

# LAURIE EVANS, CHILD THERAPIST

Laurie Evelyn Evans maintained three state licenses. In Georgia, Ms. Evans' profession was listed as Professional Counselor/Social Work/Marriage as a Clinical Social Worker, license number CSW003778. Evans' Georgia license was issued March 13, 2007, and expired on September 30, 2010, during the time of the investigation. The questionable detail on Evans' Georgia license that aroused my interest was the fact that she had obtained an examination waiver to gain her license in Georgia. Evans' license in Tennessee showed her profession as a Licensed Clinical Social Worker, license number 4473, originating on February 4, 2004; that license, too, expired during the time of the investigation, on August 31, 2010. Finally, Evans' license in Indiana showed her profession as Clinical Social Worker, license number 34003522A, approved by the Behavioral Health Board and issued on June 24, 1996, this third license also expiring during the investigation, on April 1, 2010. This indicated that Evans had been licensed for thirteen years at the time of the investigation. During our research into Evans' professional background, we identified that Ms. Evans specialized in substance-abuse counseling, family and marriage counseling, social work, and general counseling.

The purpose of this investigation was to determine if Evans had specific specialized training or education to be considered a child therapist. When looking at the specialized services that Evans offered, there was nothing listed to indicate that she had any expertise in either child therapy or child psychology. However, Evans definitely had her degree in general social work. I fired up the computer and surfed the net, gleaning information on her. On her website, I saw what she had written under one of her "specialties" profiles. Under the heading of social work, she had stated the following:

## Social Work

**Social work** is the study of social theory to improve the lives of people, groups, and societies. **Social workers** are concerned with social problems including their causes, solutions, and human impact. Their focus is to enhance the quality of life of individuals, groups, and communities by helping them reach their full potential. Social workers typically hold a professional degree in social work and may be licensed and registered.

Social workers provide a variety of services to those in need including case management (linking clients with agencies and programs that will meet their psychosocial needs) and medical social work (working with clients in hospitals, nursing facilities, schools, or hospice environments). They might work with people who are homeless, sick, disabled, or having family problems. Some social workers specialize in child abuse, poverty, violence, disability assistance, or other problems. Some social workers work as psychotherapists, counselors, or mental health practitioners.

By this loose definition of social work, a social worker could conceivably specialize in child abuse; however, as far as Evans herself went, child abuse was not listed as one of the specialized services that she offered in particular. These findings in my investigation indicated to me that Evans, even though she practiced in child abuse cases, was not a specialized practitioner/therapist for child abuse cases.

I checked not only her professional history, but what I could find about her private life. When conducting background investigations, personal information is always valuable. In doing background research on Evans, we discovered that she had been divorced, and that the divorce was not civil. (Yes, we also found out the name of her husband, but in the interests of his privacy, his name is being left out here.) Evans and her future ex-husband were married in November 2005, after having signed a prenuptial agreement. (Just to throw in a personal observation, people who sign a prenuptial agreement, in my opinion, are only anticipating their eventual divorce, which indicates a lack of trust as they are going into the marriage.)

It didn't last a year before it landed on the rocks. Divorce proceedings were initiated in 2006. Evans' ex-husband alleged that during the marriage Evans was guilty of "inappropriate marital conduct." On the other side of the domestic fence, Evans maintained that during the marriage, her ex-husband intentionally inflicted emotional distress upon her. Evans went as far as to say that due to her husband's hostile behavior toward her, she suffered from Post-Traumatic Distress Syndrome; her doctor at the time, David Solovey, PhD, corroborated Evans' diagnosis. This therapist's diagnosis of fellow therapist Evans occurred around October 2007, about eight months before Evans began conducting interview sessions with the alleged victims in the Tonya Craft case. There is no evidence about what sessions Evans had with any doctor, whether or not a doctor had released her back to work after treating her, or even if she had had to take any time off work because of her Post-Traumatic Distress Syndrome.

When finding out that Evans was diagnosed with Post-Traumatic Distress Syndrome, I began to research this disorder to have a better grasp of what her mental state likely was during the time that she was introduced to the alleged child victims. What I found alarmed me.

Post-Traumatic Distress Syndrome, better known as Post-Traumatic Stress Disorder (PTSD), is a severe anxiety disorder. I can sit here and give you my layman's version of PTSD, but for you to get the full description I have included some of the information I discovered. The Wikipedia description sums up the information about the disorder and points to the mental state of Evans before she began conducting sessions with the alleged victims in the Craft case.

> **Post-traumatic stress disorder (post-traumatic stress disorder, PTSD)** is a severe anxiety disorder that can develop after exposure to any event that results in psychological trauma. This event may involve the threat of death to oneself or to someone else, or to one's own or someone else's physical, sexual, or psychological integrity, overwhelming the individual's ability to cope. As an effect of psychological trauma, PTSD is less frequent and more enduring than the more commonly seen acute stress response.

PTSD is believed to be caused by either physical trauma or psychological trauma, or more frequently a combination of both. Possible sources of trauma include experiencing or witnessing childhood or adult physical, emotional or sexual abuse. In addition, experiencing or witnessing an event perceived as life-threatening such as physical assault, adult experiences of sexual assault, accidents, drug addiction, illnesses, medical complications, or employment in occupations exposed to war (such as soldiers) or disaster (such as emergency service workers).

## PTSD symptoms of increased arousal
- Difficulty falling or staying asleep
- Irritability or outbursts of anger
- Difficulty concentrating
- Hypervigilance (on constant "red alert")
- Feeling jumpy and easily startled

## Other common symptoms of post-traumatic stress disorder
- Anger and irritability
- Guilt, shame, or self-blame
- Substance abuse
- Depression and hopelessness
- Suicidal thoughts and feelings
- Feeling alienated and alone
- Feelings of mistrust and betrayal

## Types of treatments for post-traumatic stress disorder
- **Trauma-focused cognitive-behavioral therapy.** Cognitive-behavioral therapy for PTSD and trauma involves carefully and gradually "exposing" yourself

to thoughts, feelings, and situations that remind you of the trauma. Therapy also involves identifying upsetting thoughts about the traumatic event–particularly thoughts that are distorted and irrational—and replacing them with more balanced picture.

- **EMDR (Eye Movement Desensitization and Reprocessing)** – EMDR incorporates elements of cognitive-behavioral therapy with eye movements or other forms of rhythmic, left-right stimulation, such as hand taps or sounds. Eye movements and other bilateral forms of stimulation are thought to work by "unfreezing" the brain's information processing system, which is interrupted in times of extreme stress, leaving only frozen emotional fragments which retain their original intensity. Once EMDR frees these fragments of the trauma, they can be integrated into a cohesive memory and processed.

- **Family therapy.** Since PTSD affects both you and those close to you, family therapy can be especially productive. Family therapy can help your loved ones understand what you're going through. It can also help everyone in the family communicate better and work through relationship problems.

- **Medication.** Medication is sometimes prescribed to people with PTSD to relieve secondary symptoms of depression or anxiety, but it does not treat the causes of PTSD.

There were a few things that stood out in my research of PTSD:

1. This disorder could be caused by physical trauma, psychological trauma, or both.
2. The source of the trauma can be experiencing or witnessing childhood sexual abuse.
3. Symptoms include difficulty concentrating, depression, suicidal thoughts, and substance abuse.
4. The treatment of PTSD included exposing the person to feelings and thoughts that remind them of the trauma; It involved therapy and in some cases medication to relieve depression or anxiety

The research I uncovered answered far fewer questions for me than it raised. For instance, what are the possible implications of a therapist who is diagnosed with PTSD providing counseling to patients dealing with similarly traumatic situations? When such a diagnosis is reached, how long does it take before that therapist is then approved, to return to work? How long does it really take for a therapist who is diagnosed with PTSD to be competent and stable enough to sit down and talk to children who had been allegedly sexually abused? Was Laurie Evans the best person—or even the *right* person—to be talking to the alleged child victims in the Craft Case?

From an investigative standpoint, I considered the facts, and in my professional opinion, even though she had been in therapeutic practice for a number of years, Laurie Evans was not physiologically prepared or mentally focused to be conducting interview sessions with alleged sexual-abuse victims at that time. From further evidence I found, I was not the only one that thought this, because in December 2008 Judge Hall in Tennessee ordered Evans to withdraw as the therapist for Tonya's children—one of whom, as you know, was listed as an alleged victim. I stated before when referencing the lack of specific training of detectives Deal and Keith that the Tonya Craft case was a very high-profile, sensational case. While so many incidents in the making of this case occurred in the shadows, the legal proceedings would be unfolding beneath the watchful eyes of the public, and those who were in direct contact with the alleged victims needed to be the best experts in their respective fields, and the best that the state, or at least Catoosa County, could provide. With the emotional stresses looming in her private life at the time, Laurie Evans could not be considered as the best for this case.

# SHARON ANDERSON, SANE; CHILDREN'S ADVOCACY CENTER

Let's take a look at Sharon Anderson. Sharon Yvonne Anderson, born June 1948, was licensed as a Registered Nurse in Georgia with the Georgia Board of Nursing; her license number was RN108406, issued on November 24, 1992. Anderson, under the name Sharon Moore, obtained her certificate of completion to become a Sexual Assault Nurse Examiner (SANE) from St. Mary's Hospital and the Virginia Division of Forensic Science on August 2, 2000. Anderson attended the eight-hour Sexual Assault Nurse Examiner updated refresher course on September 12, 2002. Anderson also attended the Pediatric Forensic Nurse Training

Seminar from October 21 to 25, 2002, receiving a total of forty-three (43) hours of Continuing Education Recognition Points. During the course of the Craft investigation, Anderson was employed at Hutcheson Medical Center in Fort Oglethorpe, Georgia, beginning April 4, 1990. It was also discovered that Anderson entered into an agreement with the Children's Advocacy Center of the Lookout Mountain Judicial Circuit, where Anderson would conduct Sexual Abuse Medical Examinations on child abuse victims referred by either law enforcement or child protective services. The examinations took place at the Children's Advocacy Center in Fort Oglethorpe. The agreement was signed by Sharon Anderson RN, SANE, and Ione Sells, Director, CAC-LMJC, dated on September 12, 2008. This agreement indicated two issues:

1. Sharon Anderson was a contract employee.
2. The date on the agreement showed that it was signed after Sharon Anderson had conducted the examination on the alleged victims.

The issue with Anderson being a contract employee practicing medical exams raises some questions of professional ethics. At the time she was under contract, Anderson was also in business for herself, which means she needed to get the proper business license and general liability insurance coverage that business owners are required by law to possess before they do business in Georgia or most any other state. Since the Children's Advocacy Center is a state agency, it fortunately falls under the Open Records Act. So I requested more information about Anderson's professional history:

Children's Advocacy Center
Lookout Mountain Judicial Circuit
510 North Thomas Road
Fort Oglethorpe, Georgia 30742
April 6, 2009

**Re: Open Records Act**

Dear Custodian of Records:

I am sending you an open records request pursuant to O.C.G.A. §50-18-70 for the Children's Advocacy Center, Lookout Mountain Judicial Circuit, operating policies and procedures on cases assigned to Case Workers as it relates to assigning case numbers, notification of cases to detectives, notification of cases to the media and notification of cases to the District Attorney as it relates to child molestation and child aggravated sexual assault cases.

I request all Children's Advocacy Center, Lookout Mountain Judicial Circuit, policies and procedures for investigating child molestation cases and child aggravated sexual assault cases.

I request the Children's Advocacy Center, Lookout Mountain Judicial Circuit, required and minimum training standards for Case Workers assigned to child molestation cases and child aggravated sexual assault cases.

As you are aware, the County has three (3) business days to respond to this request. Obviously, if there are any charges for the gathering of the documents relevant to this request, I will gladly pay the same.

Thank you for your prompt attention to this matter, and I look forward to hearing from you soon.

Very truly yours,
Eric D. Echols, CFI
The LPS Group, Inc.

The Children's Advocacy Center wasted no time in responding. The very next day, I received the following e-mail in my in box:

Mr. Eric D. Echols, CFI
1050 East Piedmont Road
Suite E-134

Marietta, Georgia 30062
April 7, 2009

Dear Mr. Echols:

   Enclosed are the records requested per your correspondence of April 6, 2009. We do not investigate child abuse cases, only provide services to children referred to the CAC-LMJC.
   I am enclosing job descriptions for the positions that offer direct services to children referred here. Only the clinician position is staff; the SANE nurse and forensic interviewer are contract. Also enclosed is our Interagency Agreement with referring agencies. If you need further information, please contact our center.

Sincerely,
Signed by Ione Sells
Executive Director


   One thing I learned about sending an open records request: it's a lot like fishing. What you catch really depends on the type of bait you use. The bait, in this case, is the precise wording you put into your request. An open records request is just that, a request; it's not a search. You don't cast out a big net, yank up everything that's out there, and then cull out the trash and keep the largemouth bass and red snapper. That would be great for me and any investigator—but that isn't the way it works. You don't toss out a name and get a basket of facts; if you are not specifically detailed as to exactly what information you are requesting of them, the information, documents or data you need will not be sent to you. But on the other hand, the truly great thing about open records requests is that you can send as many as you want.
   After I sent the request dated April 6, 2009, I began to think about any disciplinary actions Ms. Anderson may have received that could have bearing on the Craft case and also whether anyone else who didn't appear on my list for one reason or another may

have conducted examinations of the alleged sexual abuse victims. So I sent another request on April 7, 2009. Below is the request. (The first names of the alleged victims have been omitted.)

Children's Advocacy Center
Lookout Mountain Judicial Circuit
510 North Thomas Road
Fort Oglethorpe, Georgia 30742

**Re: Open Records Act**
Dear Custodian of Records:

I wanted to send you an open records request pursuant to O.C.G.A. §50-18-70 for the Children's Advocacy Center, Lookout Mountain Judicial Circuit, operating policies and procedures on medical examinations as it relates to child molestation and child aggravated sexual assault cases.

I request Children's Advocacy Center, Lookout Mountain Judicial Circuit, to produce the names of those personnel that performed any medical examinations on Henke, Lamb, and McDonald in the case *The State of Georgia v Tonya H. Craft*.

**I'm in no way requesting the results or findings of the medical examinations.**

I request the personnel file including any and all disciplinary investigations, disciplinary actions, training and performance reviews, referencing those personnel that performed any medical examinations on Henke, Lamb, and McDonald in the case *The State of Georgia v. Tonya H. Craft*.

I request the required and minimum training standard to perform medical examinations in child molestation and child aggravated sexual assault cases handled by your office.

As you are aware, the County has three (3) business days to respond to this request. Obviously, if there are any charges for the gathering of the documents relevant to this request, I will gladly pay the same.

Thank you for your prompt attention to this matter, and I look forward to hearing from you soon.

Very truly yours,
Eric D. Echols, CFI
The LPS Group, Inc.

In the response letter to the second request, dated April 20, 2009, the Children's Advocacy Center stated the following:

Mr. Eric D. Echols, DFI [*sic*; should have been CFI]
1050 East Piedmont Road
Suite E-134
Marietta, Georgia 30062

Dear Mr. Echols:

Attached is the information you requested in your April 6, 2009, correspondence regarding our SANE nurse. If you wish to contact Ms. Anderson directly, here is her address: [address omitted here for privacy]. If you wish Ms. Anderson's telephone number, you should contact her by the address given.

Ms. Anderson has had no disciplinary actions through the CAC-LMJC. Her performance has met or exceeded expectations. If you wish information regarding her position at Hutcheson Medical Center you should contact them directly.

Sincerely,
[Signed] Ione Sells
Executive Director

The open records request and response from CAC-LMJC provided me with information to further my investigation on the CAC-LMJC to determine if all the policies and procedures had been followed to the letter during the Tonya Craft case. While on the surface, the letter from Sells seemed a glowing recommendation, reading between the lines told me an important point: technically, Anderson was not an employee of CAC-LMJC. This was a semantic sidestep that seemed offhand, but could be quite significant—especially if there was a feeling on Sells' part that a little distancing after the fact might be necessary. *In any office-bound culture, CYA springs eternal,* I thought, and smirked. The rest of the message gave them even more comfortable space; if I wanted any information on Anderson, I would have to go and get the information from Anderson herself. I was irked—I had wanted to find out more on this pass. However, the policies and procedures that were sent would prove to be very useful down the road.

A second issue of concern was the document that I found while researching Anderson. It was dated September 12, 2008, and signed by both Anderson and Sells. Titled "Memorandum of Understanding," it was an official agreement between Sharon Anderson, RN, SANE, and the Children's Advocacy Center of the Lookout Mountain Judicial Circuit. This document was produced from the open records request I sent on April 6, 2009. Had there been a document with an earlier signing date, that other document would have been sent. However, according to the document sent per the open records request, Sharon Anderson was not even in an agreement with CAC-LMJC to perform any Sexual Abuse Medical Examinations on child abuse victims. If this was the case, Anderson should not have been conducting the examinations on the alleged victims in the Craft case under the jurisdiction of the CAC-LMJC. Anderson also worked for Hutcheson Medical Center, but there was nothing found in my investigation that any of the alleged victims were taken to Hutcheson Medical Center for examinations.

By now you know that Ringgold, Georgia, even when you take into account the surrounding Catoosa County area, is very small. Ringgold's population hovers just above two thousand, but you couldn't tell it from the town's rambling, rural layout. Roads meander along with stretches of forest or field between houses. With the inhabited areas so spread out, it's kind of like a hill-bound Hooterville on *Green Acres*, but with newfangled conveniences like cell phones and cable TV. You'd think that a place like Catoosa County would be a good place to get away from civilization, but with so few fish in that pond, there's no anonymity. Everyone knows everybody else, and usually everybody else's business, too. But even considering this interconnected human web, I detected another pattern beginning to weave through the evidence as connections began to tie in…

What I found next raised more ominous thunder on my mental soundtrack: it turned out that Anderson was also the Deputy Coroner for Catoosa County. I leaned forward, my "a-*ha*" face lit by the computer screen. You can believe that this particular bit of information piqued my investigator's senses. Here was another sign that could, potentially, point to the inner circle,

Dwayne Wilson, who is married to Sherry Wilson (one of the original initiators in the Craft case), was coroner of Walker County, which is about thirty minutes or less from Catoosa County. This means that Sharon Anderson at some point most likely spoke with Dwayne Wilson about the Tonya Craft case as well as talked about the details of the examinations of the alleged victims.

There is something called "a preponderance of evidence," which often is used in civil cases. What this means is that evidence such as testimony or demonstration supports a claim. The amount of evidence will vary per claim, realizing that evidence is comprised of things that are either presumed to be true or proven via real or hard evidence. Here is an example: It's probable to presume that two coroners in small, adjoining counties (one of which the biggest child molestation case in Georgia has occurred) have talked to each other about the case and examinations of the alleged victims. Now the real or hard evidence would be the cell phone records, home phone records, and the coroner's office phone records to prove that Dwayne Wilson and Sharon Anderson talked to each other, how often, and for how long. Granted, I'm using a civil case legal standard with a criminal investigation, but after all, common sense does set in at some point during a criminal investigation. Do I have real evidence about which they talked? No, I do not, but in an investigation, your gut often points you in the right direction; just ask any experienced private investigator or police detective about that. I had my suspicions—but I realized full and well that that's all they were. I had no concrete proof. But still, almost anything could be a possibility, and I couldn't discount anything out of hand. I looked at the cluster map I had scribbled on the notepad: circles with *Deal*, *Wilson*, and *Anderson* written inside them orbited around a circle at the center labeled *TC*. Scribbled arrows from each outer circle flowed to the others in a circuit of logically possible connections, with the three of them focusing in to the center circle. I looked at the three arrows stabbing at Tonya Craft's circle and considered this new angle. I couldn't just dismiss this idea as being just a crackpot theory until I found evidence to the contrary. Too much seemed to fall into place when links like this were put together for me to ignore it.

I noted this evidence as a possible area for further investigation, and moved on. But I kept coming back to this theory again and again. During my investigation, it became more and more apparent that not only was it possible that the people involved in Tonya's case had a hidden agenda—but could the agencies have one as well? As I said, having a suspicion was one thing; confirming this to be fact was another. I needed to rule out the possibility that the agencies involved in Tonya's case had some sort of calculated interest behind their actions. So it was time to begin to investigate the agencies.

When conducting an investigation on an organization or agency, it's not the person running the organization that is main source of your investigation but the policies and procedures of that organization or agency and the relationships or personal connections that the key people (directors, president, etc.) have with anyone on the defense side of the case.

## FOUR POINTS, INC.

The other agency I looked at was Four Points, Inc., located in LaFayette, Georgia, in the Lookout Mountain Judicial Circuit. The Four Points, Inc., website describes itself as "a nonprofit agency offering services associated with the legal system to families involved in change due to domestic violence. Domestic violence in the state of Georgia includes spousal abuse, elder abuse, and child abuse. The services offered by Four Points are intended to aid each individual family member in coping with the changes as a result of any abuse within the family unit and their subsequent involvement in the legal system, either civil or criminal." As I could determine, the role of Four Points, Inc., in layman's terms, is to maintain a connection within the family. This means helping an alleged victim to connect with her mother, and a person who has not been proved guilty to connect to a daughter. Obviously, the goal of Four Points should have been to reconnect Tonya with her children. I do agree that due to the nature of the allegation that this reconnection should have been under supervision. But I knew that despite Four Points' involvement in this case, there had been no reconnection attempted on the behalf of Tonya and her children. It was crucial to my investigation to obtain all the policies and procedures of Four Points, Inc., as well as talk to the person in charge to undercover the reason why the reconnection with Tonya and her children did not take place. The person I needed to speak with was Ms. Melissa Gifford, Executive Director of Four Points, Inc.

On April 6, 2009, using the Open Records Act, I sent a request to Ms. Gifford asking for a copy of the agency's operating policies and procedures. I also requested the training standards for those case workers assigned to child molestation cases and child aggravated sexual assault cases. Here is the actual request I sent Four Points.

Four Points, Inc.
P.O. Box 1212
LaFayette, Georgia, 30728
April 6, 2009

**Re: Open Records Act**

Dear Custodian of Records:

I wanted to send you an open records request pursuant to O.C.G.A. §50-18-70 for the Four Points, Inc., operating policies and procedures on supervised visitation, and denial of supervised visitation.

I request the Four Points, Inc., required and minimum training standards for Case Workers assigned to child molestation cases and child aggravated sexual assault cases.

As you are aware, the County has three (3) business days to respond to this request. Obviously, if there are any charges for the gathering of the documents relevant to this request, I will gladly pay the same.

Thank you for your prompt attention to this matter and I look forward to hearing from you soon.

Very truly yours,
Eric D. Echols, CFI
The LPS Group, Inc


After the required three days had expired, I began leaving
messages for Gifford. Nearly two weeks later, on April 13, 2009, I
received a call back from her. The longer than expected wait time
annoyed me, but I didn't show my impatience; instead, I poured on
the well-mannered charm. I designed the conversation to solicit
information from Gifford about the operations of Four Points, Inc.,
without identifying my client, and I was amply rewarded. There is
an old saying "You can catch more flies with honey than with
vinegar," which means if you are nice to people, they will most
likely give you what you want, and at this time I wanted Gifford to
just talk about Four Points. Our conversation took almost thirty
minutes. Yes, of course I recorded the conversation. When I was
done talking to her, she responded to me with the email below:


**From:** Melissa Gifford
**Sent:** Monday, April 13, 2009 12:22 PM
**To:** Eric Echols
**Subject:** Four Points info

Monday, April 13, 2009

Mr. Echols:

It was nice to talk with you today. I attach what I think you will find
most pertinent. I think this should cover what we talked about. I
attached the Table of Contents in case there was something I
missed.

I know you cannot tell me much about your client but I did want to
say that we try to bend over backwards to help folks understand this

process. Even though supervised visitation is not the strange, new animal it was when I started, it is still something that I think folks are unclear about and a little scared of. I stress to all my people to be friendly and do what can be done to make clients feel comfortable. Every case is different even though there may be similarities. We strive to treat our clients with respect and listen to them and what they need from this process. And, it is a process. When you asked about length of time here, I talked about how long it takes to get through court. But, the longer the family is here the more comfortable they become and we begin to see the "true colors." It's a strange outcome of the process that I did not expect when we started doing this service.

Lastly, we are here for the kids. After working and specializing in domestic violence, I realized that the children love their parents no matter what and we can't just cut the contact with the parent and it be healthy for the children. There has to be a way to handle and deal with any abuse that may have occurred in the family. So, we take the position that if we can make the visits work and it be safe and healthy for the children we will do that. But, make no mistake, we will not allow any behavior to occur that will be harmful to the children. We don't put up with any games – from either party – custodial or visiting.

If you have any more questions, please feel free to give me a call or shoot me an email.

Thanks!

Melissa Gifford
Executive Director
& DVTF Team Coordinator
Four Points, Inc.
P.O. Box 1212
LaFayette, GA 30728
706-638-1555

With this e-mail, I received all the policies and procedures of Four Points, Inc. Now it was time to familiarize myself with this information and compare it to the information provided to me by Tonya. From the time she was arrested to this time, which was about ten months, she had not seen her daughter—and I wanted to ascertain why. After receiving all this information, I contacted Tonya to inform her about what I had obtained. Informing the client is paramount in our industry. It lets the client know you are working on the case, lets him or her know what you have discovered, and most importantly, there is the chance that mentioning some name or event might jog the client's memory and result in new information to add in the investigation. By this I mean that each new step can get the client to talking, either adding more details or realizing things had not happened the way which they had been originally remembered. Throughout this book so far I have refrained from showing you e-mails and correspondence I shared with Tonya Craft, mostly because the majority of the e-mails are protected under attorney-client privilege. However, the email below that Tonya sent directly to me, illustrates Tonya's remarks had a bearing on this issue.

**From:** Tonya Craft
**Sent:** Monday, April 13, 2009 5:38 PM
**To:** Eric Echols
**Subject:** Re: Four Points info

What did they say and who did u talk to? They refused me the right to see my kids when a court ordered them to. Joal and the therapist are pointing fingers at four points. I did everything they asked me to do. They do not have the right to deny me that because "Joal or Laurie Evans" told them so. Also it was told to me that the four points lady, Michelle Gifford, sent my info to Chris Arnt, who told her to do this and why? I went through an awful 2 hour interview where I was called a child molester multiple times. I wonder if Mr. Dewayne Wilson ever contacted them

You can see by the date that I received Tonya's e-mail right after I spoke to Melissa Gifford and then to Tonya. Tonya's e-mail clearly states that she wanted to see her children, and that she had reason to believe that Joal Henke, Laurie Evans, and Chris Arnt apparently were stonewalling, effectively denying her request. When you look back on the television news clips about this notorious case, the words *conspired* and *conspiracy* were frequently used. These words are often treated as the exclusive domain of the paranoid, of people who see everything as if the whole world were out to get them—but another old saying comes to mind: "Just because you're not paranoid doesn't mean that they're *not* out to get you." It was becoming increasingly clear that something must be going on in the Tonya Craft case—something that smacked of conspiracy in the truest sense of the word.

I have to tell you, to get the true meaning of *conspiracy*, I looked up the word, and here is what I found:

**conspiracy** *noun*
1. An agreement to perform together an illegal, wrongful, or subversive act
2. A secret plan or agreement to carry out an illegal or harmful act, especially with political motivation; plot
3. An agreement between two or more persons to commit a crime or accomplish a legal purpose through illegal action
4. A joining or acting together, as if by sinister design
*(definition by the Free Online Dictionary)*

Throughout my investigation, I determined that there were indeed individuals who were conspiring to prosecute Tonya Craft; but it was surprising to find an organization like Four Points, Inc., involved in something like this, especially in light of its stated role being first and foremost all about family reconnection. I knew what their code called for and that their policies of client treatment were not practiced or followed in the case with Tonya, which added value to my investigation. But I needed some evidence to support my suspicion or "conspiracy theory." As a private investigator, I needed to maintain professionalism and produce the facts.

I spent several days of reading the policies, procedures, and directives for Four Points, Inc., that had been sent to me by Melissa Gifford in her capacity as executive director of Four Points. When I finally closed the file and updated my case notes, I was fully prepared to call Gifford back and discuss these policies and procedures as they related to Tonya Craft.

On May 15, 2009, I punched the *record* button and had another phone conversation with Melissa Gifford. What was different about this conversation was that Gifford, without me having to say a word about it, now knew that I was private investigator working on behalf of the Tonya Craft team. What she made of this, I don't know. The whole basis of my contacting Four Points was because I still had some questions about how her agency had handled its role in facilitating the reconnection of the alleged child victim (Tonya's daughter) and the alleged perpetrator (Tonya herself). Four Points, the agency recognized by Lookout Mountain Judicial Circuit to fulfill this role, seemed to be doing an irregular job on this one. And I wanted solid answers as to why the Craft Case met with such irregularity.

In particular, I was attempting to find out why Tonya was not allowed to see her children from the time she was arrested on June 8, 2008, through the time a court order was issued disallowing Tonya any visitations with her children, which was in December 2008 / January 2009. During those five to six months between these incidents, Tonya could have seen her children. In fact, during that time, she *should* have been seeing her children, but she had not been allowed to.

It was a legitimate question for Four Points. Repeatedly during that window of time, Tonya had asked to see her children, and all requests had been turned down out of hand. Someone there at Four Points must have known the status of the case and that there had yet been no ruling handed out that would forbid Tonya from contact with her kids.

What was key to me during this conversation with Gifford was the fact that it had been the opinion of child therapist Laurie Evans that was the deciding factor why Tonya was denied any contact with her children during this five to six-month period. Gifford replied to the effect that when a therapist is involved in a case of alleged child abuse, Four Points talks to that therapist to determine if a reconnection is going to happen. They take into account the overall details and facts of the case along with the responses of the children. In fact, Gifford stated that Evans had informed her that Tonya's children said they did not want to see their mother. Gifford continued by stating that Evans further stated that it was in her opinion that allowing a reconnection with their mother would not be in the best interest of the Craft children.

Let's stop here for a minute: Remember that it was Laurie Evans who was ordered to stop the sessions with the children by Judge Hall in Tennessee; it was also Laurie Evans who was diagnosed with Post-Traumatic Distress Syndrome prior to her sessions with Tonya's children. While Gifford was prattling on about how much she respected Evans and valued her opinion as a therapist, I was glad I was on a phone so I didn't have to keep my poker face on. I rolled my eyes to heaven and shook my head when I heard Gifford's glowing report about this woman. As a professional private investigator (and I know I have stated this a time or two), no matter what I believed personally, ethics and professionalism prevented me from asking Gifford whether she was crazy. Did she really not know, or was it a case of not *wanting* to know what was up with a therapist in her employ? Either one indicated Gifford had a less-than-firm hand steering that agency, to say the least. I resisted the strong impulse to tell her what I knew about the real Evans. Hearing what Gifford told me during this conversation and knowing what had been discovered thus far in the investigation, it was beginning to become clear that regarding the dispensation of Tonya Craft and her children, Four Points, Inc., was operating solely on the information that was provided by Laurie Evans; any concern about the mother and children who were victims of this situation was beside the point.

What also stood out in this conversation was the fact that Gifford stated she had talked in person to Chief District Attorney Chris Arnt, but when I tried to pinpoint the timeframe and circumstances of their encounter, she could not remember where exactly she had spoken to him. The conversation Gifford had had with Arnt was specifically in reference to Tonya reconnecting with her children. Gifford added that there was an official meeting about the reconnection, but she was never notified as to the conclusion and the results of the meeting; therefore, in her words, she "left it alone."

*Left it alone*? Melissa Gifford is the executive director of Four Points—what, did she just throw up her hands and leave it at that? Her offhand characterization of her action was difficult to believe. So, as the head person in charge of an agency dealing with at-risk families and mounds of red tape and forms, where was her follow-up? Come on! This was a legal case! Didn't that mean that she had a duty to be accountable on this particular case?

This suspicious evasiveness indicated to me that there could indeed have been a decision to let Tonya reconnect with her children—however, it was not important enough for a follow-up call. From my perspective as a private investigator, the facts I was discovering were falling into a pattern that told me something unusual was going on with the Tonya Craft case.

There was so much sneaky maneuvering going on that I had to nail some of this jello to the wall using their own language. With the information supplied by Gifford, it remained my job to look at everything that had transpired with Four Points and find a concrete procedural reason as to why they felt justified in denying Tonya access to her children. This research specifically included going back to Four Points' policies and procedures to see if anything was written stating or directing Four Points to take the opinion of the therapist as the deciding factor not to allow reconnection. It was not surprising that I found nothing to that effect written in Four Points' policies and procedures. I went through their policies and procedures front to back and back to front and back again, and I found nothing. Their procedural protocols didn't address basing the decision whether to grant visitation in child abuse cases on the therapist's findings.

What I did discover was a policy titled "Sexual Abuse," marked as "Special Cases Policy 5:2." This policy begins with the line *"Cases presenting with an allegation of sexual abuse...*" I want that phrasing to sink in, but right now, let me just point this out: while it was my job to find information to aid in the defense of Tonya Craft, this is not meant to minimize the gravity of this crime. Sexual abuse of children, in this author's/private investigator's mind, is by far the most evil, immoral, wicked, horrific act that a person can perpetrate. I say this because children are innocent and trusting; to prey on a child is the basest act an adult can commit. With that perspective in mind, let's go back to the specific wording of that document's opening statement:"*Cases presenting with an allegation of sexual abuse...*" It is stated in this manner because in our justice system (and when I say *our* justice system, I mean it in the sense that it belongs to everyone in the United States of America), the concept of presumption of innocence is a cornerstone of our legal system. The principle that a person of any persuasion is automatically considered innocent until proved guilty is embodied in several provisions of the United States Constitution. So until a person is proved guilty of and is convicted of a crime, that individual is otherwise presumed to be innocent. When an agency such as Four Points implements a policy addressing sexual abuse, it can refer to it only as the "allegation of sexual abuse." Without a legal ruling, the presumption of innocence dictates the wording of this. But the entire wording of the first sentence demonstrates an important point: "*Cases presenting with an allegation of sexual abuse will be maintained at the severe level of supervision until the allegation is unsubstantiated.*"

Let's consider this. This is addressing a hypothetical situation in which sexual abuse may have occurred, laying the groundwork for continued interaction between the abusing party and the victimized minors. Hell Yeah! I totally agree a "severe level of supervision," as Four Points worded it, should be maintained to protect the child! But Tonya was denied even this rigorously supervised degree of contact with her children, despite the fact that she had not been proved guilty—but according to the policy that was in place, the question of the accused guilt is beside the point. I have included the policy for you here so you can see yourself. I challenge you to read this without getting the creeps...

| **Special Cases** | Issued by: Executive Director | Policy #:**5:2** |
|---|---|---|
| | Prepared by: Executive Director | Revision #: |
| | Approved by: Board of Directors | Effective Date: 6/1/2006 |
| Subject: **Sexual Abuse** | | Page **1** of **1** |

**Policy:**

Cases presenting with an allegation of sexual abuse will be maintained at the severe level of supervision until the allegation is unsubstantiated. Any substantiated case of sexual abuse, such as a criminal conviction, will remain on severe supervision level throughout services here.

Two staff members should be present in the building during such visitation.

At no time during the visit should the visiting party be left alone with the child(ren). The following restrictions will be in place as well:

* Children should be dressed in pants or shorts. No skirts or dresses for girls.
* Children should be dressed in shirts or clothing that covers their back and abdomen.
* Children may not sit in the visiting party's lap, wrestle or

roughhouse with them.

* Visiting party may not aid the children on the swing sets by pushing in swings or lifting them up in the air to get on ladders/slides/etc.

 * No photos or videos can be taken of the children without express permission from staff after consultation with referral source and other service providers for the family.

**Rationale:**

The child involved may be afraid to visit with the parent fearing that the abuse will happen again. The presence of staff in the room with the child will make the child more comfortable and prevent the abuse from happening during a visit.

Research tells us that certain things can be catalysts for an offender to offend. By restricting the alleged or convicted offender, we protect the children from victimization.

With the help of computers, pictures can now be used in many ways. Seemingly innocent pictures can be used in child pornography. Consultation with others involved with the family allows a knowledgeable decision to be made.

That's right—you read it there, step by step. Four Points' own policy made room for a person with the allegations of sexual abuse to reconnect with the child victim or alleged child victim. The rationale given in their policy is that *"The child involved may be afraid to visit with the parent fearing that the abuse will happen again,"* clearly showing that Four Points, Inc., understood that it was routine for visitations to occur between a confirmed minor victim of sexual abuse—and the human piece of shit who had put that whole family in that emotionally wrenching pit in the first place! I was sick to my gut as I read their "protective rules." And yet, even though their policies on reconnection had a lot of latitude built into their own rules, the door was slammed shut in Tonya

Craft's face. She was physically kept away from her children during the last few months she might ever have been able to see them. Based on the conversations I had with Gifford, e-mail correspondences, and Four Points' own policies and procedures that were not followed, my investigative conclusion was that certain forces conspired against Tonya to prevent her from seeing her children.

Those forces, as identified in my investigation, were Laurie Evans, child therapist; Sharon Anderson, SANE; the Children's Advocacy Center; and Melissa Gifford, Executive Director of Four Points, Inc.—these three women were also all connected to Chief District Attorney Chris Arnt, a trail leading back all the way to the influential one who had the ability to pull their strings. These women were all in positions of authority and trust which entailed behavior of a higher caliber of human being; yet individually, if not collectively, all three of them either violated ethics by making decisions based on personal bias and opinions rather than on professional findings, or by circumventing and not following their own policies and procedures when dealing with Tonya—all in an apparent effort to satisfy Chief District Attorney Arnt's needs in securing those twenty-two headline-grabbing guilty verdicts against Tonya.

# As The Plot Thickens

The fact that all this behind-the-scenes jerking-around had the double effect of tormenting Tonya by not allowing her to see her children made their efforts even more cruel and callous. By the same token, those kids had been kept away from their mother, and as far as I could tell, they had no doubt also been brainwashed against her.

As much as I didn't want to go there, I had to think in that direction because that was where the evidence was leading me. There were too many of these interconnected official stonewallings to be coincidental: the conversation with Gifford led me to believe that there was a concerted plot afoot in the works. Someone was directing things and pulling official strings to make sure Tonya did not see her children—and what I was uncovering was fitting the classic definition of a conspiracy.

At every turn I could see a concerted effort by multiple players to achieve the same baffling goal: to accuse this woman of a hideous crime that she wasn't guilty of, multiply it by twenty-two times over, and then railroad her into prison, all because of—of what? *What?* What possible benefit was there to gain from persecuting this particular woman? Tonya Craft didn't have money, or influence; she was a kindergarten teacher, not a target that needed taking out. There was no tangible motive for all of the chicanery and secret double-dealing—and the very center of it, the core of the matter, this whole ugly mess was over nothing! *Nothing*, I reflected, *but bitter, small-minded spite*. That was about the size of it. It was out of sheer spite that this fortress of bull got built, brick by lying brick—spite and mendacity, like a standard Southern soap opera. I flashed on *Cat on a Hot Tin Roof* with Burl Ives as "Big Daddy," glowering in disgust and growling, "Didn't you notice a powerful and obnoxious odor of mendacity in this room?"

Old Burl was right—the lies stank to high heaven. I was searching for the truth, but I was soaking in lies, and I was sick to damn death of the stink and the stench that laid lingering about.

It's part of my job not to throw off signals, to keep control and stay above the game, unaffected and objective. Maintaining an exterior that was cool and professional had become my default setting. But the further I investigated this case, I became aware that beneath the surface my blood was beginning to boil. As an American—and as a human being—I became more and more appalled and disgusted with the justice system in Catoosa County. But I swallowed it down, deep, and held my contempt inside. Knowing what I knew, I couldn't help but look down on cavalier disregard of the Catoosa County justice system and those "certified professionals" in name only who had sworn oaths to protect the innocent and especially children. But I was too much of a professional to give in to my feelings—giving vent to my anger would only be counterproductive and impair my investigation, so I did not let the other members of the Craft defense team see or hear my disgust, nor did I let my disgust affect the job I was hired to do. In fact, there were times during this case when tempers flared and nerves were worn ragged. But whenever my clients yelled or got angry, I just sat there and remained silent rather than spill out my real feelings and further complicate already complicated matters.

As the case wore on, it wore all of the people on the Tonya Craft defense team out—especially Tonya Craft. The times we were face to face, I noticed how Tonya looked more and more worn and frazzled—and indeed, she couldn't hide the fact that she was emotionally raw. She was doing a damned good job of holding up through this horrific ordeal—I mean, think of it! Could you live anything like a normal life with this much heavy, *heavy* stuff hanging over your head while you're cut off from those you love the most? Man, that is a terrible road for anyone to have to walk. And this woman was trying to keep her chin up through all this and act like nothing was wrong, when in her life, *everything* was wrong. Everywhere she turned, she was being jerked around and tormented like a pawn in an ugly game of tug-of-war. It would be a rare person indeed who doesn't crack under the stress in a situation like this. But unfortunately for Tonya, she wasn't that rare unaffected exception. The emotional turmoil was taking a toll on her.

There were many times I observed Tonya going through different stages of a rolling breakdown. She tried to hide it behind forced cheerfulness, but the cracks were showing more and more in the face of the dam. Or maybe a volcano would be a better metaphor, because under these stresses she was just an emotional pressure-cooker ready to erupt. There was no particular favorite target when she went off; it was a matter of being in the wrong place at the wrong time. All it took was a casual mention of some trigger word that inadvertently tapped into all that repressed hurt and anger, and **POW**, she'd lash out and let you have it, no matter who you were. It had gotten to a point where everyone else on the team was getting gun-shy. But as I have mentioned a couple of times, I'm a Marine. There's no such thing as an ex-Marine—I didn't think I'd face combat on this job, but my experiences in the Corps made me ready to face anything.

The rest of the team learned to duck and cover, but that didn't help the cause of the outburst. So I dealt with it by presenting myself as the focus for her rage, to help her dispel some of it, get it out, and get to where she could think clearly again. You learn the warning signs when you're working in a volcano zone: her façade would begin to break. And I could tell the anger inside needed to escape for a moment, and I'd look her in the eye and say, "OK, I'm 'it.' Bring it, I can take it," and just stand there impassively while she railed and raged and got it all out. This became a familiar dynamic between us, almost like therapy. I wasn't getting a penny of extra pay for it, but I was doing multiple duties as an investigator, an interviewer, a bodyguard, a psychiatrist, and a verbal punching bag. With the amount of anger she must have had inside, I'm surprised she didn't physically punch me during her spells—but when she got wound up, that polite Southern lady could practically take the paint off of the walls. It didn't happen a lot, but when it did, it was like a force of nature that we all just reckoned with, and understood. That being said, there was this one time in particular that I'm going to talk about here—because later, during Tonya's trial, District Attorney Len Gregor attempted to make inflammatory legal hay out of this incident.

In September 2008, I was in Ringgold doing interviews for the case. I was only going to be there for two days, the 9th and then later the 27th. These were both very long days; as I was the

Certified Forensic Interviewer on the case, I was the one doing all the interviews with the witnesses and potential witnesses for Tonya's trial. Due to the sensitive nature of the interviews, both for their content and for legal reasons, meeting at the McDonald's on Old Alabama Road was out of the question, somewhere private to conduct these interviews was needed. It was decided I would conduct these interviews in one of the meeting rooms at a local hotel in Chattanooga, Tennessee. It was close enough to Ringgold, but it gave us some comfortable distance—or so I thought.

The defense attorneys Scott and Cary King were in attendance, as was Tonya. Also present was a professional legal consultant hired by the Kings to assist them in sizing up potentially good defense witnesses during the trail. But the lawyers and the hired gun weren't there to ask any questions; they were just there to absorb the information that my questioning would elicit from our candidates. I was the one who would be conducting all the interviews. Let me just say that to be in the company of all those college degrees—not to mention all the years that Scott and Cary had under their belts in trying criminal cases—and to be the one entrusted to do the interviews...? That gave me a truly sweet feeling of achievement, knowing that I was appreciated and respected by those on the team. Please don't misunderstand—this wasn't a special case that I went all-out on just this time. Far from it. I had always done good work for Scott and Cary King, as I had on many other cases. But the Tonya Craft case was an incredibly high-stakes gamble, and everyone had to be on their "A game," *plus.* I had expected high-caliber ringers to be called in once it got to the deeply legal nitty-gritty, but they chose me for this crucial stage of the process. This just demonstrates how the team all had confidence in my abilities and skills in conducting interviews.

Let me take time out and talk a little about the interview process during this case. During the actual interviews, it was me, the person I was interviewing, the videographer, and the court reporter in the room. A complete record was made of all my questions and the answers I got in return. One by one they were led in, and the process began: they sat down and settled in, then I went through the list, varying the order and delivery of the questions as suited each potential witness, as well as asking my own questions and my own follow up questions to their responses. We'd wrap up, then another contestant would be ushered in: they sat down and settled in, then the process started again... Again and again and again and a break for lunch and *again*...

Afterward, as I looked back at my reports and listened to the numerous audio and video recordings I had obtained during those two days of intensive questioning, I noted that I had conducted a total of thirty-six witness interviews on behalf of the Tonya Craft team. Some of the people I interviewed were potential witnesses for the defense, potential witnesses for the prosecution, and just some people who knew the key players in the case.

Out of all the people I interviewed, I'm going to talk in detail about the one interview subject whose acquaintance I valued the most. Kimberly Walker, a true LADY! At first glimpse you could tell Kim was the type of person with good ol' Southern values and morals; the type of person that would put the welfare of others before herself, showing the unselfishness of a saint; the type of person who believes in the true meaning of wholesome family living and showing pride in her upbringing—a lady who believed in and practiced truthfulness, fairness, and compassion, extending her grace to all people. Kim Walker, a true lady—and I do mean *lady* in all the senses of the word!

Kim was one of the Ringgold moms who knew Tonya Craft, believed her, and testified on her behalf during the criminal trial. In my opinion, Kimberly Walker was the one witness who strongly aided in the acquittal for Tonya. I found her to be, credible, and most of all HONEST, so much so that I conducted two interviews with her. The first interview I conducted with Kim Walker was on September 27, 2008, at the hotel in Chattanooga, Tennessee. Kim was on the list of other potential witnesses I was slated to interview that same day. But what I heard from the other interviewees paled beside what Kim revealed that afternoon. Till this day, her words make me shake my head and think, "*Surely, not in today's society...!*"

She was shown in and sat down on the edge of her seat, looking alert and eager to share what she knew. I just figured from her body language and forthcoming answers that she was the perfect interview subject—I had no idea that this interview was going to be the smoking gun it turned out to be. Because Kim gave me an account on how, just after the allegations against Tonya had come out, she had been contacted by Sandra Lamb. I leaned forward at the mention of that name, believe me; but I caught myself and disguised my move by reaching for my water as Kim went on. Sandra Lamb had called her up to inform her that she would be getting another phone call soon. (*Just like a little psychic friend,* I thought sourly.) Kim listened as Sandra helpfully explained to her how she'd just happened to have heard that Detective Deal and Assistant District Attorney Chris Arnt were going to be calling. They wanted to talk with Kim about her own daughter having been molested by Tonya.

My thought at this point was how the hell did Sandra know Kim was going to get a call from Deal and Arnt? Then I started conjecturing that there could have been some discussion between Deal and Arnt and Sandra about other alleged victims. If they wanted to go on a fishing expedition, Sandra Lamb knew where all the likely fishing holes were, and it looked like a baited hook was tossed in the direction of Kim Walker to see what they could reel in.

During this interview, Kim stated that she was contacted by Arnt as Lamb had foretold her. Arnt told her it couldn't be handled over the phone, that she had to bring her daughter in to talk to Detective Deal. Kim stated she took her daughter to Family Services, where they were met by detectives Deal and Keith. Kim was ushered into a waiting room and told to take a seat, and then the detectives brusquely whisked her daughter away to an interview room before the startled mother could react. Kim described how she attempted to follow them, but was blocked at the door and prevented from entering the interview room to be with her six-year-old daughter, even after she asked to be admitted.

Let's take a moment and picture this! So, here you have a six-year-old little girl who's standing there with her mommy, when suddenly two big police officers, most likely wearing their guns on their belts right at a child's eye level, take her by the hand and lead her off to a room without her mother being present. Put yourself in the parent's place in this equation for a moment: If your six-year-old daughter were taken off by two big, scary cops who then barred you from entering the interview room—?! Imagine the thoughts that would seethe through your head if you couldn't listen to how they were talking to your child and hear what they were saying. Now, let's all take a moment and calm down, because I know what you are thinking! No way in HELL!

I could just imagine the scene when the door finally opened and the scared child almost ran into the arms of her mother. The detectives walked out of the room, looking down with blank expressions at Kim as she protectively held her little girl close. Afterward, the detectives told Kim that in their interview, her daughter had stated to them that nothing inappropriate had happened with Tonya Craft; however, recordings of their interview with Kim Walker's child never surfaced. I found out during my investigation that it was a procedural requirement that police interviews with children be videotaped. Also, it is a basic legal right of the parent(s) to review the videotape of the interview with their child or children. I asked her about this fact, but Kim stated she never was allowed to see the video—even after calling the Catoosa County Sheriff's Office and requesting to view it. Kim told me that she had been told by the Catoosa County Sheriff that because it was part of an ongoing investigation, she could not see the video interview of her daughter. I do understand the need for the protection of evidence in ongoing criminal investigations, but from what the detectives themselves had stated, Kim's daughter had reportedly denied the allegations that any inappropriate behavior by Tonya had occurred. I have to say, a six-year-old girl holding her own in a room with two detectives only meant to me that this scared child was telling the truth, loud and clear. This innocent little girl's statement of truth was pointed to the lies that someone had spread condemning Tonya—and that someone was Sandra Lamb.

The second interview I conducted with Kim Walker was on March 30, 2009. This time, the interview was conducted in her home, where I could study Kim in her natural surroundings. She met me at the door, smiling and pleasant, and invited me inside.

Kim's home was a picture of southern country living, very well kept with charming country décor touches. I could tell she took as much pride in her home as she did her own appearance. Kim waved me past the living room, saying, "Let's talk in the kitchen," and led the way to a neat, well-appointed kitchen/dining room. Now let me say this. The kitchen has always been the place where I was accustomed to spending most of my family time as a child, and it still is till this day. It's like the heart in the house, a place of openness and comfortable ease, a less-than-formal atmosphere. As I began to set up my video-recording equipment on the sparkling clean kitchen table, Kim looked past me toward the sink and let out a little disappointed sigh. "Oh! Please excuse the mess," she said.

I looked around to see what she was talking about. "What mess?" I asked—and then noticed a few dishes sitting in the sink. That was it! But to her, that was enough to constitute a disgraceful mess! I had to laugh out loud at that one. "Ma'am, that is no mess, believe me," I assured her.

She laughed kind of nervously as if I were being far too polite. Then, in a quaint country drawl, Kim asked, "Can I offer you some water?" As I said before, a true lady!

The purpose of this interview was to follow up the accounts that Sandra Lamb had made in her deposition. Part of my assignment was to go over the depositions taken by the defense attorneys of the Craft team. This was an important role, due to the fact when any person—well, for convenience's sake, let's make it *you*. When you give a deposition, your responses should be truthful, since what you say during a deposition is under oath. A deposition given in a lawyer's office is every bit as legally binding as testimony delivered in a courtroom—so binding that what you say in your deposition can come back around to bite you and be used against you later during a trial. In theory, during a deposition, if you are not truthful, avoid questions, make up answers, or just sit there on your butt and lie outright, well, that's *it*, —you can go into court later and tell all the truths you want, but your weaseling acts during your deposition will count against your testimony as not being credible.

So when I had the opportunity to review Sandra Lamb's deposition, I scanned that document for what I suspected I could find there, and I noticed that there were multiple answers by Sandra referencing Kim and her child. Even though a person should tell the truth during a deposition, this is not always the case. I couldn't take this witness's word at face value, not by a long shot. I had to cross-check everything that came from this horse's mouth, so in order to validate Sandra's deposition, I decided to conduct another interview with Kim.

Preparation before conducting an interview is key to the success of obtaining the information you want. As an example, while reading Sandra's deposition those questions asked by Tonya's attorney and the answers given by Sandra—her interpretation of the facts gave rise to a multitude of questions from my perspective. As I read her depo, I took pertinent parts of it and kept a running list of questions for answers that I wanted to get, with the intention of running them past Kim Walker. You can see what I mean in the following excerpts from the transcript of Sandra's deposition. [*NOTE: In the interests of privacy, the children in this sequence will be identified only by surname—and in between the pertinent excerpted bits of Lamb's deposition testimony, my questions for Kim will appear in bold italics with bullet points.*]

In the first excerpt, she had been asked to describe the "writing on the ground" incident, and this is what she swore to.

## Excerpt from Sandra Lamb's Deposition:

**LAMB:** [*The Lamb daughter and Wilson daughter*] were walking around their pool. [*Kim's daughter and the McDonald daughter*] had been swimming, and they were riding bikes or trikes or something around the pool and writing with sidewalk chalk, and Sherri and I were on their deck watching, just looking down. And [*the Wilson daughter and Lamb daughter*] said, "Mommy, come look at what [*Kim's daughter*] wrote." And we went down there or I didn't at first, and Sherri asked her daughter what did it say, and her daughter told her. And Sherri was like, "*What?!*" And she went down there and looked, and then I went down there and looked.

## My questions for Kim Walker:

- At the Wilson home, when you where told about the writing on the ground, who told you it was your daughter who had written the words?

- Exactly what words were written there on the ground?

- When you arrived to pick up your daughter, did you see the writing?

- Could you tell by the way it was written that you daughter had written it?

## Excerpt from Sandra Lamb's Deposition, continued:

**Q:** Okay.

**LAMB:** And Sherri asked Kim's daughter where she had heard that.

**Q:** And what did she say?

**LAMB:** And she said from Tonya's daughter.

## My questions for Kim Walker:

- When you talked to your daughter, did she say that Tonya's daughter told her those words?

- Did your daughter say if the Lamb's daughter and/or the Wilson's daughter had told her to write the words?

- Did you daughter say which child actually had written the words?

## Excerpt from Sandra Lamb's Deposition:

**Q:** Okay. And then what?

**LAMB:** And Sherri said that I'm going to have to tell your mommy and daddy when they pick you up, and like right after that my daughter and I left to go home. Later that night, I don't know what time, Sherri called me—Wilson—and said that she had talked with Kim and her husband—and they were absolutely—from—I don't know what they were. They were not—they were mortified, from what I understand.

## My questions for Kim Walker:

- When you talked to Sherri Wilson about the "writing on the ground" incident, did you describe how you felt?

- Where you ashamed, embarrassed, horrified, humiliated, offended, or anything of the like?

- Did you express any of these feelings or other feelings to Sherrl Wilson?

- If so, how did you express these feelings, and what did you say?

- So, if someone were to say you had been "mortified," would that truthfully characterize your reaction to the incident at the time?

## Excerpt from Sandra Lamb's Deposition, continued:

**LAMB:** ...and Kim was upset because she—they had recently had Tonya's son and their son, at a—Kim said this—at a Mexican restaurant, and Tonya's son was—there was a picture of a female, and he was pointing and rubbing the breasts of the picture, and then Kim's daughter said the "sex" and "kissing."

## My questions for Kim Walker:

- Do you remember, during the time of the allegations prior to the "writing on the ground" incident, when you took Tonya's son and your son out to a Mexican restaurant?

- Who else was with you there?

- Did you witness any inappropriate behavior by any of the boys?

- Did you witness Tonya's son pointing and rubbing the breasts of a woman in a picture and then your daughter saying "sex" and "kissing"?

- If someone said that you had told them that this incident had actually occurred, would that be the truth or a lie?

- Did you tell Sandra Lamb that this incident with the boys had occurred?

## Excerpt from Sandra Lamb's Deposition, continued:

**LAMB:** So on—from what Kim has told me and what Sherri Wilson told me, on the way home, Kim and her husband started questioning their daughter.

**Q:** Their own child?

**LAMB:** Their own child.

**Q:** Okay.

**LAMB:** And from what their own child said—and I talked to Kim on Saturday morning. From what their own child said, I began to question my daughter more because it was more than what my daughter had said in the beginning.

## My question for Kim Walker:

- Did you call Sandra Lamb and tell her that your daughter told you anything that would suggest that any inappropriate behavior had been committed on this child by Tonya Craft?

## Excerpt from Sandra Lamb's Deposition, continued:

**Q:** What was it that they told you that Kim's child said?

**LAMB:** Kim's daughter had— They asked their daughter where she learned the words about sex and kissing, and she said Tonya's daughter. And she said, "How did you learn that?" and she said Tonya's daughter always wanted to play girlfriend and boyfriend. And Kim said—I don't know what she said after that, because I know the next thing—she continued to question her daughter and her daughter said she—you—also taught me to touch in inappropriate places.

## My questions for Kim Walker:

- Did your daughter tell you where she learned the words "sex" and "kissing"?

- Who did she say told her those words?

- Has your daughter ever told you that she played "girlfriend and boyfriend"?

- Did she say who she played "girlfriend and boyfriend" with?

- Did she explain how this game is played?

- Has your daughter ever told you she has been touched in inappropriate places?

- If so, where on her person has she been touched, and who touched her?

- If anyone stated that you told them that your daughter told you any of the following statements, would that be the truth or a lie...?

    ...that it was Tonya's daughter who told your daughter about the words "sex" and "kissing"?

...that Tonya's daughter always wanted to play "girlfriend and boyfriend"?

...that Tonya's daughter has touched your daughter in inappropriate places?

This was just an example of the research I did on Sandra's deposition to prepare for the second interview with Kim Walker. I did the same for everyone who was deposed in the case, as well as developing follow-up questions for those individuals who were going to be deposed a second time.

During the interview, Kim Walker told me that it had been her daughter that wrote the word "sex" on the ground at the Wilson home that afternoon at the party when all the children were playing. Kim stated she got a call from Sherrie Wilson, who was upset because the children had been playing unattended, and someone had discovered that one of them had written "sex" on the driveway in chalk. Kim stated that she told Sherrie she was en-route to pick up her daughter anyway when Sherrie had called. What piqued my interest at this point in the interview was that fact that when Kim arrived to get her daughter from the Wilson residence, Sherrie Wilson told Kim that if her daughter had been with Tonya or Tonya's children, then she needed to talk her—implying that something inappropriate must have certainly happened if Kim's daughter had been alone with Tonya. Kim also talked about how Sandra called her on the phone multiple times very adamant about what she needs to do with her own daughter. Kim stated that Sandra was quite insistent, saying that if she did not bring her daughter in to talk to the police, that the police would come to the Walker house and take the child in for questioning. Keep in mind that everyone who knew Sandra Lamb also knew her connection and influence with the police and the DA, so Kim believing that the police or sheriff was going to come and take her daughter away was not farfetched. That was when Kim voluntarily took her daughter to the police, and the ensuing incident occurred where her daughter was taken away and questioned.

During this second interview, Kim also told me that yes, her daughter had admitted to her that she and Tonya's daughter had fondled each other while playing the "girlfriend and boyfriend" game. Kim stated that she was shocked that had been going on and told her daughter sternly to stop playing that game. She was concerned enough to have consulted her daughter's doctor over it just to make sure that the girl hadn't been injured in some way. After an examination of the child, the pediatrician concluded that there was nothing physically wrong with her daughter. Kim denied that Tonya's son had been rubbing and touching a picture at the Mexican restaurant, but she did say one of the boys had looked at the picture and giggled and said, "Boobies." Kim stated she never told or talked to Sandra about the incident at the Wilsons' or claimed that she was "mortified." In fact, Kim stated Sandra was calling her so much over this that she got to the point that when her cell phone started ringing, she just let the phone go into voice mail to avoid that harping voice.

I was trying to remain the impassive interviewer, but it was hard not to chuckle at someone getting rubbed the same wrong way by that woman. And the "boobies" remark, I have to admit, kind of made me grin. Childhood is a time of innocence and wonder—and also a time of social one-upsmanship, when the child next door who knows something that the other children don't is the one who rules the neighborhood. I can attest to that because, as hard as it is to imagine—long before I was a private investigator, long before I was a Marine—I was once a little boy. I can remember the way children  acted when they start noticing the differences between males and females, the way everything is suddenly fascinating and secret— and *everything* sounds like it could be dirty as all get out. Like that time in fifth grade when the teacher mentioned the book *Moby-Dick* and a hush fell over the students—and then Marcus in the back row couldn't hold in his laughter and the whole classroom erupted in pandemonium along with him. That's the way I remember it, from longer ago than I'd like to admit.

But look at the culture we're soaking in today—from day one, children are being bombarded with sexualized content in everything from cheesy reality shows to music videos to soda commercials, for heaven's sake. They don't understand it as sexual, though—it's more like a flashy shorthand for being an adult. From the evidence I was gathering, a counter theory began to come to light. What I was hearing about the behavior of the kids here was messed up, yeah—but it didn't sure didn't add up to evidence of molestation. It looked to me like this scenario could be explained as a case of way too much unsupervised media exposure and some appallingly lax parenting. Whatever inciting force caused these incidents, it sure didn't necessarily point to Tonya Craft. But someone had a dislike of Tonya Craft, and that otherwise minor personality conflict had bloomed into a witchhunt.

Kim Walker stated that she had never believed the rumors and lies that were swirling around about Tonya Craft. From what she knew, Tonya had never done anything inappropriate with her daughter. Furthermore, Kimberly Walker told me that she also had believed that the same was true of Tonya's behavior with the other alleged victims—in fact, at the time of the interview (March 30, 2011), Kim was still allowing her son to play over at Tonya's house. When Tonya finally had visitation with her son, Kim's son even stayed the night on sleepovers.

I did ask Kim if she had received any calls from Detective Deal or ADA Chris Arnt. She stated she did get a call from the Sheriff's Office requesting to re-interview her daughter again. There was a confident tilt to her chin as she went on to say that she had refused to submit her child to that ordeal again. After that contact, she did not hear from the Sheriff's Office again about the matter. I thought of the way Kim's little girl had refused to fold, even when they were trying to break her. All I could say is "like mother, like daughter"—I was proud of the way both of these Walker women were holding their own. Now you can see why I respect Mrs. Kimberly Walker so much and call her A True Lady!

Now back to the interviews … Sometime at the end of the day during the course of the interviews I was conducting in Chattanooga on September 27, the attorneys left the hotel heading back to Atlanta, Georgia, as I finished doing the interviews. After the interviews were completed, Tonya and I decided to go get something to eat—a routine decision with any of the clients I have. After a grueling day, dinner and drinks are a good way to unwind, and the conversation can often give you new insights and leads. I called my wife Patricia to fill her in on the day's results and to let her know I'd be on my way home after taking our client out for a meal.

On the way to the restaurant, I made a comment to Tonya. "Watch and see if we run into someone who knows you and this case."

Tonya gave a tired *who-cares* shrug and replied, "It's just dinner." Sure, it was only that—dinner between a client and the private investigator on her defense team. And we were up in Chattanooga, TN, so it narrowed the chances that we'd run into someone. But we've seen how some of the players in this case can take the truth and make sausage out of it. And I was walking into a grinder.

We strolled in as normally as any two people would walk into a restaurant, Tonya entering first as I held the door open for her. As I came through the door behind her, I could feel all eyes on us. At first, I thought to myself that people must be staring because they recognized Tonya from the TV news. What with Ringgold being right in its backyard and Tonya's photogenic appeal, the Tonya Craft case was becoming big buzz in Chattanooga.

But meanwhile, the big buzz in the restaurant had hushed. Yeah, Tonya must be the reason, I rationalized. But I knew I was telling myself that because I did not want to think it was because Tonya is a white woman and I am a black man. But as I surveyed the room and saw the narrowed eyes and dropped jaws, a movie image was replaying in my mind: Remember the scene in *Blazing Saddles* when Cleavon Little arrives in Rock Ridge as their new sheriff, and the celebrating townspeople all suddenly go from rowdy and boisterous to stone-cold silent in a heartbeat? I couldn't help thinking of that. That—and the fact that this is the freaking *twenty-first century! Come on*, people!

So I just did not mention anything to Tonya. I tried to look as blasé and professional and unthreatening as we were seated, but the unthreatening part was beyond my control. So I brazened it out—but before I could even unfold my napkin, I heard Tonya hiss at me across the table. "Over there," she breathed, looking behind me. "It's David. My husband."

At the time, Tonya and David Craft were separated and talking about a divorce because of the molestation allegations. The divorce from Joal Henke had been painful enough for Tonya to endure, and here she was, with all this legal action hanging over her head, with another doomed marriage looming on the horizon. "Uh oh...!" She was staring over my right shoulder, unable to look nonchalant. "Here he comes...!" She grimaced.

But I had already spotted him. I could see his reflection in the mirrored wall opposite me, which is why I chose that seat. An ordinary-looking man, about 5'10 185lbs, reddish hair with grey highlights, casual dressed, manicured goatee, nothing flamboyant about him was approaching me from behind, making a bee line for our table, but he wasn't making any overtly threatening motions. Looking rangy in a polo shirt and Dockers without a jacket, I could see that he obviously wasn't packing a weapon. I kept my posture relaxed but ready as David Craft casually walked right by our table in a very slow, very significant way. He did not say a word, but turned his head and looked right at me—a challenge I thought, but it was too weak to be nearly invisible. I could see him trying to make what he no doubt hoped was a fearsome game face, but he succeeded in only looking peevish. Then he continued right passed us to the restroom.  This was surely a walk by to see who Tonya was with and to size me up, because after about fifteen seconds David came out of the restroom.

As I watched David Craft's movements, I felt like an anthropologist in the field: This was obviously some territorial display of rural yuppie manhood, like an ape beating awkwardly at its chest and then loping off. This was turning into a hill-country soap opera, with Catoosa County standing in as a low-budget Peyton Place—and I did *not* want to get mired in that kind of personal mess.

I started to excuse myself to hit the restroom to wash my hands before we ordered, and Tonya waved me to bend close. "Do me a favor," she whispered. The favor was a request for me to do a walk-by near where David was seated to check and see if he could be on a date with another woman.

*Oh, man...!* I let out a tired sigh at the idea of someone else's sticky romantic intrigues, but I had to acknowledge, what if he was with some of the other players in this case I thought, so there I was headed to the other side of the restaurant to complete my task. This other side is also where the bar was located and the direction David Craft had headed back to after his fly-by. There was nothing covert about this walk by. There was no concealment, not to mention I was the only black in the joint. As soon as I walked nearby, David's entire table looked at me. All I could do was nod at them, and go to the bar. While at the bar, I got the attention of one of the employees, asked him a question and proceeded back to my seat.

But when I returned back to our table with the reconnaissance report that David was not running around with a women, he was just out with friends, I figured this was good news for Tonya. Out of nowhere, Tonya had decided to break down anyway over David being out. The idea of him running around had already got her dander up. I guess it felt so good to get mad at something other than the case that she wasn't about to give it up now that she had a good head of steam going. I could tell she wanted to storm across the restaurant and give David a big ol' piece of her mind, and that was the last thing I needed to deal with on top of everything else. I was talking fast, trying to convince her it was not in her best interest to confront him in a public place, especially now, what with her trial coming up ... but I could see my words of caution were falling on deaf ears. Tonya was a boiling teakettle about to go off LOUD, and I knew right then and there that it was high time to leave the restaurant. Wouldn't you know the waiter was finally approaching the table to take our orders, but I was already rising up out of my seat to go. "Sorry," I told him, and waved him off. "Never mind—we are leaving." And we got up and left.

Or rather, *I* got up—

—and then I dragged the angry Tonya Craft the hell out of there as subtly as I could.

This is an example of what I mentioned earlier—that if you were around Tonya during a meltdown, you were the one that caught it. Man, did I ever! It was a misjudgment on her part (to put it lightly), but what stoked it was the issue she had with her yet-undivorced husband over loyalty. Tonya felt that out of respect for this terrible, unjust ordeal she was going through, David should not be out on the town in Chattanooga. Whatever her reasoning, this was a potential problem with any client, and my response was by the book. It was my job at that time to be proactive; to do damage control *before* the client could do any damage. I deflected her ire by giving her battered ego some props, telling her in a low voice how she was a great mother and a wonderful lady, and assuring her that she would triumph over the lies—all while getting her the hell across the floor, through the door, and out of that restaurant. It was somewhere between *Dancing with the Stars* and a fireman's carry.

Looking back on this incident, by itself, it's almost funny. I could see that same scene, but set in a dark-paneled old chophouse with a squabbling New Jersey mob family and played for laughs—but like I said, that's looking back on it. At the time, it wasn't funny. It was something that happened despite my attempts to avert the crisis, and when it began to spin out of my control, I dealt with it as fast and as best I could. If you are a private investigator, please remember this: you can show empathy and understanding while still being professional. But empathy only goes so far when the client is about to say or do something to compromise the case; when you are protecting a client in an investigation, that includes protecting the client from themselves, if necessary. Sometimes a situation threatens to become so volatile that boldly decisive measures are the best alternative—often the only choice you have. Call it Marine reflexes, but I reacted fast, and it worked.

Considering the risks the entire case would have run if I had let that situation develop, I felt like I'd avoided a disaster. But despite my efforts at containing it, Tonya's eruption still created a memorable public snapshot. And when this same picture was analyzed from a different perspective—one with a definite agenda pushing it—it would be painted differently. Hell, by the time they got done with it, their picture of that incident would be a total whitewash.

I was going to find out all about it—but that would be later. Looking back now, I wish I could have let myself know that all this craziness was actually the calm before the storm. Right then, I was too busy staying knee-deep in B.S. to appreciate that idea.

This job was taking a toll on me. Even before having to physically drag our client like furniture, I had been doing all the heavy lifting with the investigation, but now I was wearing so many hats I felt like a hat rack in Macy's Department Store on Black Friday. I was getting the stink-eye from the powers-that-were, no doubt sizing me up for a rough ride once this case hit the courtroom. It wasn't my first time at the rodeo; I was prepared for harsh scrutiny and hardnosed attitudes. If you are going to work on a high-profile criminal case for an extended amount of time, you will need to have a thick skin. You may have to take some ridicule or withstand some attacks from time to time. But the questions are—how much will you have to stand? And how far will they go to break you?

So far I had logged two years on this case, and I showed no signs of breaking. In that time, I had shown the Craft defense team and everyone I had faced in this investigation, that yes—I had developed some damned thick skin.

But that was beside the point: what mattered most to the power structure of Catoosa County was the color of that skin. And no matter how thick it would prove to be—they wouldn't quit until they saw it bleed.

# The PI Becomes the Pawn

Catoosa County was a rinky-dink little place, and in its rinky-dink little way it had put me through the mill. So far during this case, I had been slapped, called a black bastard, and cursed out— not something that would dent this Marine's thick skin, but these deplorable actions were wrong enough to be actionable offenses, and I wasn't taking them lying down. The individuals who had set themselves against me thought they were pit bulls, but it was more like being bitten to death by ducks. They were not slowing me down or putting me off the case. What I had uncovered through Jerry McDonald was courtroom dynamite. I was prepared to stride proudly into court, raise my hand and take that oath, and then testify about what I had uncovered. I knew there were people out there that had a serious stake in this whole vicious mess who wouldn't like what I had to say. Things could get ugly—as ugly as some of the behavior I faced along the way here.

Still, I was not prepared for just how ugly things were going to get for me.

It began when I walked into the Catoosa County Magistrate Court to pursue a pre-warrant hearing against Sandra Lamb. This hearing had been initiated in response to the assault on me by Sandra when she smacked me in the face. Like I said, I wasn't about to take that crap lying down. No matter how angry you are, it's not a good idea to wail away on someone that you don't like because they are doing their job. The plain and simple truth is that by law you cannot do that to others—you throw the first punch, that's your butt in a court of law. And if the other party doesn't hit back, you the aggressor are left hanging out in the legal breeze. This is a long-accepted part of American jurisprudence; the rule of law guarantees the human rights, protection, and dignity of each individual. I knew that as far as the technical side of the assault case went, the law was on my side. Furthermore, the offense had taken place under the all-seeing eye of my cameraphone, and once a jury saw that rawboned human welcome wagon in action, her behavior would speak for itself.

So, full of confidence and the feeling I was doing something right, I strolled in to file my pre-warrant application on Sandra for the assault charge—and instead got an official notification from the Magistrate Court myself. All I knew was I had walked in, come up to the counter, stated my name, and the lady there smiled and handed me an envelope with my name on it. I tore it open as the clerk was explaining how the court had just been getting ready to mail it to me, and here I was, so convenient. *Yeah, sure,* I thought, looking down to see that it was a hearing notice.

It turned out that the wheels of Catoosa County Just-Us— excuse me, "justice"—were grinding my way. Sandra Lamb had already filed a warrant application for my arrest. Well, point/counterpoint—I explained to the clerk that I was there to complete a warrant application as well. She looked up over her reading glasses, surprised, and asked if I had any evidence in my case. I explained that I did, so she got up like it was a big pain to bother with it and trudged back to the judge's chambers. After a few minutes, she trudged back with the answer: "The judge said he will review your evidence when you come back for the hearing for Sandra Lamb." I thanked her and left, ready to return on the hearing date of August 7th. I had no idea how that day would turn my life upside down...

August 7, 2009 arrived, and oh boy, was I prepared. My team met bright and early at the Catoosa County Justice Building, and we had a quick logistical review in the parking lot. With me were my wife, Patricia; my attorney, Samuel Sanders, of the law firm McCamy, Phillips, Tuggle & Fordham; and Robin Martinelli, president of Martinelli Investigations and a board member of the Georgia Association of Professional Process Servers. Mrs. Martinelli was there to give me an edge—she would be testifying as an expert witness on conducting process services, giving invaluable background details since the assault incident had occurred when I was effecting a process service on Sandra. We locked and loaded—well, actually we locked our briefcase latches and loaded our bottles of spring water for the long morning session in court. Then we turned and headed to the courthouse.

When all of us walked down the street to the Catoosa County Magistrate Court as one body, it was like a scene from a Western movie when the showdown is about to go down. We were a solid phalanx of professional talent, striding down the main street of a one-horse town to lock horns with the corrupt powers-that-be— but still, in my heart, I felt a sense of aloneness, of hanging out by myself in the breeze. Catoosa County was a damned cold-hearted place to be an outsider, and to the people who lived here, I was an outsider on more than one count.

I wasn't just set against a double-dealing legal system; the bigger foe was something that was even harder to get a grip on. It was a kind of mindset that was like a brick wall. I had seen it barefaced and raging, pouring out of Sandra Lamb's mouth like a toxic spill. That was what I was up against in this place. Here, I was through both the looking glass *and* the time machine. This whole place seemed to exist in a vacuum, simply because people like Sandra liked it better that way. It wasn't a point of if the glass was half full or half empty—I was facing people who couldn't see the damned glass in the first place. That brick-wall mindset protected them, and it was going to be an obstacle for me to overcome. And even though I didn't fit their nightmare profile of a scary psycho/thug/gangsta/copkiller they'd picked up from bad TV shows—I was fine for their purposes. In fact, a successful, educated black urban professional could be perceived as a threat here on even more levels. I wouldn't be just another person with a complaint coming before the judge to argue my case—right out of the gate, I'd have to waste some of my valuable court time just trying to demonstrate them that I was a human being so that they'd respect my argument.

I frowned, thinking about what B.S. it was that I was going to have to win them over just to obtain my rightful justice. But how? How could I connect with people who thought on such a level? How could I be accepted as being on an even footing with them? I hadn't even entered the courtroom yet, and I was beginning to feel dog tired of all this. But the one thing that spurred me on right then was not because I felt ready to go before the judge; it was not even because I knew I did not break the law. It was because of what—actually, *who*—I saw when I walked into the lobby of the Magistrate Court.

The Tonya Craft case, even before coming to trial, had become the focus of intense public interest. Fueled by the internet, word had spread about what was going on. A solid base of people formed who, convinced of this schoolteacher's innocence, came out on the side of Tonya. They kept up with the unfolding developments and showed up at the courthouse in ever-increasing numbers during different court proceedings to demonstrate their support for Tonya Craft. We had all been so glad the way grassroots support was forming for her—it really helped bolster her sagging spirits as the case wore on.

But at the same time, support had been forming for me, too. It seems my name was already well known among Tonya's supporters, because when I walked into that lobby, I saw two dozen smiling faces beaming back at me—people whom I had seen sitting behind Tonya in court, all concerned Catoosa County citizens. I was floored—I had no idea I was showing up on the radar and that people cared what I was going through. Then I turned and saw Tonya Craft's parents, Mr. and Mrs. Ferris. They, too, had turned out in a show of warmth and support for me. I must say that for a black man to have such solid backup in Catoosa County was overwhelming; it was a true blessing.

I also saw Sandra Lamb sitting in the waiting area, but her lawyer was nowhere in sight. I turned to my attorney, Sam, and whispered, "That's Sandra Lamb, but her attorney is not with her." Seeing Sandra in a courthouse without her attorney gave me pause. Let me put this in perspective for you: Sandra showing up stag at a court proceeding without her attorney is like watching a NFL football game without quarterbacks. It's like going to the Kentucky Derby and seeing the horses run without jockeys. It's like the Lakers playing in a championship and not playing Kobe

Bryant. If you understand those comparisons, you can see why seeing Sandra without an attorney gave me pause. Previously in court, she stuck so close to her lawyer that they looked like a she-he three-legged race. But today, sitting there without her hired legal gun, she looked like only half of a set.

When the bailiff called our case, he saw so many people who were not African American stand up with me that he had to ask, "Uh—all of you are for the *Echols* case?" The look he had on his face was a sight to see. I turned to look at the Caucasian faces of my crew and realized that my wife and I were the only African Americans in the room.  I didn't have occasion to think about that detail being unusual in any way. It certainly wasn't strange enough to be remarked on with a double take. Our differing heritage was beside the point—what counted was the fact that each of us was a dedicated professional. But the fact that I didn't only deal with members of my own race seemed to throw his way of thinking for a loop. He blustered that we were to follow another bailiff to the hearing room. My wife Patricia gave me a kiss for luck as we gathered our gear and prepared to do battle.

As we all filed into the courtroom, even Judge Wells seemed to be thinking, *What in the world is going on?* He looked sternly across the assembled people in the courtroom, then ordered, "If any of you is here as a witness for the case, you need to leave." Only Robin Martinelli got up and left the courtroom. The look on Judge Wells face was priceless, so much he had to ask, "Are all of you here for the Echols case?" The responses of yes and the nods of affirmation sent a chill through my soul.  All I can say is, God is Almighty!

I could explain what happened during the hearing, but it was all written out in digital type—so you can read for yourself. Below is the transcript of the entire pre-warrant hearing as it occurred that morning.

IN THE MAGISTRATE COURT FOR THE
COUNTY OF CATOOSA, STATE OF GEORGIA
SANDRA, GREG, HADEN & [*minor child*] LAMB,
Plaintiffs,
  -vs-
ERIC ECHOLS
THE LPS GROUP
1050 E. PIEDMONT ROAD
SUITE E134
MARIETTA, GEORGIA 30062
and
ERIC ECHOLS,
  -vs-
SANDRA LAMB,
XXX CLASSIC TRAIL,
  Defendant.

---

BEFORE THE HONORABLE R. V. WELLS, III, MAGISTRATE
TRANSCRIPT OF PROCEEDINGS
AUGUST 7, 2009
APPEARANCES OF COUNSEL:
For Ms. Lamb: Pro Se
For Mr. Echols: Sam Sanders, Esquire
    McCamy, Phillips, Tuggle & Fordham
    Post Office Box 1105
    Dalton, Georgia 30722-1105

BE IT REMEMBERED, that the above-styled cause came on for hearing on the 7th of August, 2009 before the Honorable R. V. Wells, III, Magistrate of the Circuit Court of CATOOSA County, Georgia, where the following proceedings were had, to wit:

**PROCEEDINGS August 7, 2009, 9:29 a.m.**

**THE COURT:** Ms. Lamb, we're here today on two different affidavits, one of them that you've signed on July the 27th indicating that you wanted to have this hearing. Now, is it your intent to try to get a warrant—

**MS. LAMB:** No, just a—

**THE COURT:** —for the arrest of Mr. Echols?

**MS. LAMB:** No, just a restraining order. Someone filed the wrong paperwork or gave the wrong form. It's simply a restraining order.

**THE COURT:** Mr. Echols?

**MR. ECHOLS:** Yes, sir.

**THE COURT:** You have also signed an affidavit indicating that you wanted to try to get a warrant for the arrest of Ms. Lamb. Now, is that your intent today?

**MS. LAMB:** And I don't have a copy of that.

**THE COURT:** Is that your intent?

**MR. SANDERS:** That was his intent at the time of the filing of this, Judge, yes.

**MR. ECHOLS:** Yes, that's correct, Judge.

**THE COURT:** Well, is that still what your intent is, to try to get a warrant for the arrest of Ms. Lamb?

**MR. ECHOLS:** Yes, sir.

**THE COURT:** Sir, your name is what?

**MR. SANDERS:** Sam Sanders, Judge. I filed an entry of appearance last week.

**THE COURT:** Sanders?

**MR. SANDERS:** Yes, sir.

**THE COURT:** Ms. Lamb, based on the fact that you are indicated as the Defendant in one of these affidavits, you do have the right to have counsel with you today. Do you want to proceed with this without counsel?

**MS. LAMB:** No, because I don't have a copy of that warrant.

**THE COURT:** Well, it's not a warrant. No warrants have been issued.

**MS. LAMB:** Right, but I didn't have a copy. Mine was just simply for a restraining order; it had nothing to do with any kind of arrest.

**THE COURT:** Do you want me to proceed on your complaint today?

**MS. LAMB:** On my complaint—

**THE COURT:** Yes.

**MS. LAMB:** —but, like I said, I didn't know the other was out, so I would like to have counsel for that.

**THE COURT:** Mr. Sanders, these affidavits, do you know whether or not they concern the same incident?

**MR. SANDERS:** It is the same incident, Judge.

**THE COURT:** Well, then, I'm not going to hear either one of them today. But what I will tell both parties: Until this does come back for hearing, I'm going to order that there be no contact between these parties. I've read the affidavits. I do understand that it appears Mr. Echols is a process server.

**MR. SANDERS:** That's correct, Judge.

**THE COURT:** Well, he's not going to be serving anything else on Ms. Lamb. He's not going to be having any contact with Ms. Lamb.

**MR. SANDERS:** Until further order of the Court, Judge?

**THE COURT:** Yes. Now, Ms. Lamb, you know that applies to you having contact with him, also?

**MS. LAMB:** Yes, sir.

**THE COURT:** Okay. Now, Mr. Sanders, is there anything else that you need to bring to my attention right now?

**MR. SANDERS:** If a continuance has been requested and granted, Judge, we don't have anything further

**THE COURT:** Okay.

**MR. SANDERS:** I mean, we would like to proceed today, Judge, but—

**THE COURT:** I understand, but if this is pending from the same incident and Ms. Lamb
is indicated as a Defendant and she does wish to have counsel, I'm going to give her that opportunity. So we're not going to hear either side of this today. But by that court order, both Mr. Echols and Ms. Lamb understand that there is to be no contact between you all—

**MS. LAMB:** Yes, sir.

MR. ECHOLS: Yes, sir.

**THE COURT:** —until we get back in here. Everybody is dismissed.

**MR. SANDERS:** Is a written order going to be issued in that regard?

**THE COURT:** It will be put on paper, but it's in existence right now.

**MR. SANDERS:** I understand. Thank you.

*[Proceedings concluded]*

Let me highlight some key points in this transcript. Within the first thirty seconds that Judge Wells addressed Sandra, she started playing fast with the truth. I had thought perhaps she'd toe the line better in court than she seemed to over the phone making late-night calls, but a change of forum didn't slow her down. From my perspective as a certified forensic interviewer, this consistent bending of the truth was becoming so routine that I wondered if it could be some sort of pathological problem. Right there, on the record, Sandra stated, "Someone filed the wrong paperwork or gave the wrong form." Yet she had completed and signed the pre-warrant application—as a matter of fact, she had added another charge on her application: "Provoking a witness in a criminal case on property of one of the victims." That's a very loose interpretation of how Sandra Lamb stormed around and screeched and snarled and yelled, and then slapped me and called me a black bastard. But the video evidence I got wasn't yet involved in the equation, so only I could appreciate the contrast. That wasn't the side of Sandra who appeared in the courtroom: this was the demure, soft-spoken Sandra, working hard to seem as innocent and vulnerable as her name implied. She looked even more *oh-poor-helpless-me* standing there alone without her lawyer. That was a big wrong note. This type of proceeding required an attorney by her side, and she and I both knew it. How could she possibly think she wouldn't need her legal firepower with her at this hearing ... unless that was a deliberate move?

But back to the transcript. There's more:

Early on in the transcript, you see where Judge Wells brings up my signed affidavit for an arrest warrant for Sandra. I acknowledged that I did, and then Sandra states she does not have a copy of my affidavit against her. Here again we see how the plain and simple truth is too slippery a slope as she claims ignorance of my affidavit. For this to be true would mean that the Catoosa County Magistrate Court had failed in its duty to send the notification to Sandra. It was the Magistrate Court who presented me my notification that Sandra had filed against me, and it was the same Magistrate Court's job to send Sandra a notification that I had filed a warrant application on her. The notification system surely hadn't been broken when it came to dealing with me; it's hard to believe it wouldn't work on her end, especially considering all her high-flying connections in the county government.

Then, again in this transcript, when she is asked by Judge Wells if she wants to proceed with a warrant issue for my arrest, Sandra states that it is not an arrest warrant she wants but a restraining order; moments later, she states again that her application is for just a restraining order and has nothing to do with an arrest—the two separate instances show it wasn't a misunderstanding. Since at this time, Sandra was not exercising her right to have legal counsel present with her, Judge Wells refuses to hear the evidence for the warrant and states he will not hear either one us, until this case comes back for hearing. Judge Wells's final order is that there is no contact between Sandra and me. Judge Wells does not rule whether a warrant would be issued. Then that's it.

I had expected to be in there fighting it out into the afternoon with Sandra and her hired legal guns— I hadn't foreseen her coming into the hearing chamber without packing some heat. So then it's *wham, bam, and sorry, it's over for now,* just like that. After all this prep we did for this morning's proceedings—and nothing, *nothing* got accomplished. Man, I hate to waste time. Time is precious, and wasting it is bad enough to be a sin, especially when the wasted time is other people's, too.

It was obvious that nothing was happening here today. As I packed up documents at my attorney's table, my stomach growled. The natural body tension of my battle-stations stance had worked up an appetite. I looked at my watch. We all had other things we could be doing, but before we went off in separate directions, I figured the team could go out for an early lunch nearby. The eating options around Ringgold were a bit lean ...

But before we could all run out to a restaurant—I ran smack face first into something else I hadn't foreseen.

As we were making to leave the courtroom, a Catoosa County sheriff deputy entered and approached Judge Wells as he was still sitting on the bench. The judge bent toward him, as he whispered something in the judge's ear. Judge Wells then looked up sharply at me and said, "Mr. Echols, wait where you are!" I felt a sinking feeling. I saw Sandra slowly stand up with a sly, satisfied grin on her face and sidle out of the courtroom, nose in the air. So much for her game face—I could tell she fully knew what was about to come down. And it was all going to come crashing down on me.

As Sandra Lamb slipped out, Detective Deal entered the courtroom. He had two other plainclothes officers and another uniformed sheriff deputy with him; they all began walking ominously toward me, as if they were relishing a struggle. This wasn't unfolding like this—suddenly the whole playing field had flipped over on me. I bent over to my attorney Sam and said in a low voice, "I'm getting ready to go to jail."

Sam looked back at me with raised eyebrows. "For what? No, you are not." By then, the goon squad had reached the table. That's when Detective Deal asked me to stand up and directed me to come with him.

All I could do was try to maintain my composure; it's not like I had a choice, being surrounded by so many officers. The door leading out the courtroom to the lobby was open. The waiting room was in view—and there she was, Patricia was craning her neck to see what was happening inside. Our eyes met and locked. This was when I needed my woman to be a professional who thinks on her feet, and I knew I had that in Patricia. She was ready to do what was needed. *What?* her eyes flashed. I shook my head and began taking off my jewelry, sending a message to her that something was wrong.

That was all I had time for. I was hustled away out of her sight and taken into a room adjacent to the courtroom. Detective Deal looked me up and down, then asked me if I were carrying my gun. So, he'd been doing his research on me and knew I was licensed to carry a concealed weapon. I responded that I didn't have it on me. I didn't, for two reasons—the first and main reason being only a damned fool strolls into a courthouse with a gun on his side.. The second reason was the plain truth—even though I'm a private investigator, I have a clean enough lifestyle that I don't need to pack heat like some *Miami Vice* fantasy. But that was beside the point right then. I was up against that brick wall in both senses of the term.

Was I carrying my gun, he asked. I said, "No, I'm not," and then I was read my rights. Once Detective Deal was done reading me my rights, I heard those words—the words a law-abiding citizen always thinks that they would never hear: *"Turn around, and place your hands behind your back."*

My only reply was "You have got to be kidding me!" What the hell is going on here? This wasn't happening—everything felt surreal and shifting, like I was in some kind of strange *Twilight Zone* limbo. Physically, I knew better than to resist, but as I felt the chill steel of a handcuff circle my right wrist, my mind was silently arguing the point: *I'm not the guilty party, I'm the good guy, I had the law on my side—the law, all printed out in black and white...* The left cuff clicked shut as the irony closed in—the kind of black and white where they basing this move on had nothing to do with the law. Here, there was no law. The law would only get in the way of Catoosa County justice.

I straightened up and turned to face Deal. I might have been shackled, but by God, I was *not* going to bow down to these men. I stood proudly, calling on my ingrained Marine bearing. Deal glared up at me, trying to look tough. I returned his stare, impassive and unblinking. Then, as he looked me square in the eye, Detective Deal stated:

"This is from Chris Arnt."

Plain as freaking day: *"This is from Chris Arnt"*—that was what Detective Deal said. If I hadn't already been holding myself back, at the sound of those words, they couldn't have pried me off him. It was everything I could do to keep my cool. But the message was clear.

"This is from Chris Arnt."

Those words were making my mind race. Deal had delivered the message like a hit man's line in a cheap gangster flick.

I could take Deal's comment in two different ways:

1. Chris Arnt was letting me know that I was now in his county and he was in control; or

2. Detective Deal wanted me to know that he did not agree with me being arrested and was only doing what he was told.

Either reason you want to go with still makes it smack of an unethical abuse of power. This little love note also served to send an unspoken message to me that Chief District Attorney Chris Arnt was willing to do whatever he wanted to spike the ball on those twenty-two guilty verdicts against Tonya Craft—even if it meant arresting an innocent man.

I have always known and believed, since I was a child, that if someone commits a crime against you and you follow the law by the book, then it is your right to notify the police or sheriff and have that person arrested. But if you have never broken the law—if your daily routine is to go to work, do your job the best way you know how, perhaps (if you're lucky) help someone in the process, and at the end of the day know you have been blessed to live this sweet life—you would never expect to be arrested. But as I heard the familiar words of the Miranda Act being recited to me, I was stung by the irony in the repeated phrase: "*You have the right … you have the right … you have the right …*" Like *hell* I did. At that moment, to these men, I had *no* rights.

August 7, 2009, was the day I stopped believing that justice and our legal system was fair. In fact, I started believing that justice and our legal system was a business, and like a business, it could be bought, traded—or bartered for a favor. All it took was for Detective Deal of the Catoosa County Sheriff's Office to say, "Put your hands behind your back," followed by him slapping those stainless steel bracelets on my wrists. When those cuffs clicked shut behind me, that hard metal *snap* echoed through me like a rifle shot. "*No, no, noooo…*" I thought wildly, "*This is not happening to me!*"

I know you've heard that line before in movies. It's an old cliché, the part in a novel where the character thinks, "This is not happening to me!" But that's exactly what was running through my head. Being arrested like this was the last thing I ever expected to experience. To explain where I'm coming from, you should know where I've been.

I told you early in this book about how I started out, but that didn't get into the *why* of me. Growing up in a broken home in the inner city of Detroit meant that as a little kid, I had to get acquainted fast with things nobody should witness. I have seen abuse up way too close and way too damn personal. Not just physical abuse, of which I've seen plenty, but something even more damaging, a kind of beat-down from the inside that doesn't show the scars—the abuse of power, the cruel domination of another human being's soul. It's bad enough when adults play out that game on each other—but it seems there's always some poor kid caught in the crossfire.

The worst part is a child is naturally in the weakest position of power to start with. They don't understand the most basic truths in life. They don't have any idea what "normal" is. They're looking for some kind of direction, and if there's nothing but a blank outline where a parent should be, that lost child is left with an empty, painful place inside that he wants filled more than anything. But whoever comes in to fill that vacuum also has the whip hand, the hand of power. No adult starts out a new relationship with a blank slate. There's a whole lot of messy baggage and issues that get dragged along into it. Children want to love and trust—but when reaching out only results in drawing fire, any poor child gets all twisted up inside. It's like mental daggers facing inward, stabbing at every turn. The child sometimes grows into a fearful, unhappy adult who takes out everything on himself.

But in some cases, that emotional hurt goes the other direction—and when those mental knives point outward, it's *"Screw the world! I'm gonna hurt it worse than it's hurting me!"* And the world pays for it in robbery and murder and all the other nice things human beings shouldn't do to each other.

But in a few lucky cases, something else fills that empty vacuum, and the broken child's life turns in another direction, an upward one. In a world of disorder, he finds something that has the power to set things right. Something like law and order becomes a surrogate father influence, and the child's desire for authority and guidance is transferred to outlets that are socially approved.

Going by my background here, try to guess which one of these paths I took: in elementary school, I was Captain of the Safety Patrol; in high school; I took a Protective Services class taught by the Detroit PD; and at seventeen, I went into the Marine Corps, where I served as an MP and Security Force in the Infantry. Then, after I was honorably discharged, I did loss prevention and security for almost thirty years, and in 2003, I formed The LPS Group, Inc. My chosen path through life was on the side of good. I had found my own sense of security by guaranteeing the security of others through my private detective agency. I rose through a system I have admired, upheld, and followed to the letter all my life, doing everything by the book, to the point where I was handling cases for the office of the Attorney General. With so many strikes against me, I had become an upright man who made his family, his mama, and his pastor proud.

And here I was in handcuffs, surrounded by a clutch of small-town cops who were swelling their chests and smirking at me like they'd caught Dillinger or something. It didn't matter that I was on their side—my simple presence had been enough to antagonize them, pushing buttons in them that I had nothing to do with. I would find little sympathy here. This part of the country had a long history of removing people of color who stood against them— Chief John Ross of Rossville had learned that the hard way. From the looks of their strutting around, the good ol' boys here were about to send me on my own trail of tears. I pushed down my rising anger and just tried to go with the motions for now until I figured out what I could do.

I was acutely aware of the cold steel handcuffs locked around my wrists as I was handed over to another cop for the next step in this ordeal. It was a familiar face, at least. I recognized Officer B. Dowis as one of the officers who had been in the courtroom when Tonya went to court for motion hearings. We walked to the police vehicle, and I stood beside the patrol car while Officer Dowis opened the door. I felt totally feeble being unable to open my own door. Then, as I was getting in the backseat, I felt the creepiest sensation—! It was a hand on top of my head. "Watch your head," Dowis said and guided me in. He had clapped his hand onto my head as he placed me in the car, as if I were some ninny who might bash his own brains out on the door frame! I burned inside, and tried to swallow my frustration before it showed on the surface.

I settled into the back seat, trying awkwardly to sit like a human being without crushing my hands, which were still bound behind me. Dowis made sure I was all in, and then he shut the door. It wasn't a hard slam, but in my mind, the sound of that door closing echoed like Dracula's vault slamming shut. I was shut tight in there, too. That car was soundproof; I could see the cops talking, but I couldn't hear a thing. It was like being underwater. I felt like I was drowning. Sitting in the back of a police car is the most embarrassing, demeaning, and belittling experience you can have. It's like it's made to be uncomfortable—I mean, there's not even any leg room. Everything seemed deliberately designed to humiliate the arrested party, from the absence of inside door handles to the presence of the steel cage divider. I looked around the cramped space and shuddered despite the August heat. I looked out the window to see if I could see a friendly face, a supporter would be nice I thought, no one was seen. I was alone, feeling defeated and broken, but I would be damned if I let those Catoosa County sheriff's see it.

Then Officer Dowis came back and slipped behind the wheel, and the squad car pulled out. I clenched; I was on my way to whatever hell was waiting for me. At least my people knew where I was, I thought with a small degree of comfort. They had seen me taken away against my will, so I couldn't just disappear without questions being asked... Despite my situation, I smiled at the dramatic turn in my thinking there. It wasn't like Dowis was going to pull off on a dirt road like in one of the 60's exploitation cop movies. You know the ones I mean, where they kill me execution-style and hide my body up in the hills here. But that was the point. I had offended people with the power to screw up your life so much you'd wish they'd had the balls to kill you. And the way I lived and worked, this arrest classified as killing me.

All I could think about was that my life was over, and the justice system in Catoosa County was going to lock me up and throw away the key. It was like a knife in my heart that this system that I felt I was a part of had become warped enough to turn on me, one of its own. The law I loved was dragging me away from my wife, my life, and everything I knew, and I was helpless to fight it. When my thoughts turned to Patricia, I had to swallow the bubble of emotion that almost choked me. I love my wife, and I have utter belief in her abilities under pressure. I knew whatever was going on with me, my woman had my back and right then was already taking care of business for me. Patricia is brilliant, focused, capable, and totally together, and she's at her greatest under combat conditions. I knew she'd come through for me—but she was probably just as scared and uncertain as I was right now, and I couldn't be there to reassure her because I was stuck in the back of a cop car! It was like a kick in the manhood to realize that. *I* was put on this earth to protect *her*. I wanted nothing more right then than to wrap my arms around her and tell her everything was going to be all right. But that was an impossibility, because with these handcuffs on, I couldn't hug anyone—and as for making everything all right, that was entirely out of my control. It was like I was trapped inside the looking glass on the wrong side of it, and I couldn't get out.

As I was being transported along the winding road to the Catoosa County Detention Center, Officer Dowis turned to look at me and dropped the second cryptic remark of the hour: "It seems you got yourself in a spider web."

His perfect assessment of my situation startled me. That surely was the God's honest truth! I *was* trapped in a web—a web designed to trap just me, one that had been spun by Chris Arnt and his good friend Sandra Lamb. I could see them as big, ugly, hairy spiders, smacking their greedy fangs as they crawled down to devour me. Oh yeah, I was stuck in a web, all right—but to hear this fact acknowledged straight from the mouth of one of the arresting officers bowled me over. I looked back at him, trying to read his face for any extra clues as to his exact meaning. His expression was cool, but something in his eyes seemed sympathetic. I nodded in agreement with his remark and replied, "Yes, it seems that way." Boy, was that a colossal understatement.

As I have mentioned, I have interviewed upwards of a thousand people for felony crimes over the past twenty years and I have learned over the years to interpret body language and other giveaway signals in an interview subject. But that was when I was cool and collected, and on the other side of the table. I couldn't

totally be sure which end was up right then, but that statement—
*"It seems you got yourself in a spider web"*—indicated to me a
strong possibility that Dowis knew I was only being arrested
because of my involvement in the Tonya Craft case. But that wasn't
enough to go on—I couldn't tell for sure if that was his meaning. I
ran it through my head again: *"It seems you got yourself in a spider
web..."* I sure hadn't been expecting compassion—but his tone
hadn't seemed like sarcasm.

Too soon the patrol car pulled up at the Catoosa County
Detention Center. Officer Dowis got out and opened the door for
me. It was like having a chauffeur, except a chauffeur usually
doesn't have to help his boss squirm out of the backseat without
using his hands to get leverage. When we both got me to my feet,
he escorted me into the jail. When we got inside the doors, we
went to the intake center where I was to be officially booked and
processed. I stood there, cuffed and feeling humiliated, as Dowis
leaned on the counter and gave the rundown to the officer who
was taking the inmate processing information. The other intake
officer in the room shot me the stinkeye from the protection of his
desk—not to mention from behind his badge. I was trying to
suppress my rage, but I felt it begin to surge up, and the longer
that guy glared at me, the more I began to see red. But I forced my
anger back in the box before it slipped out and compromised me
further. I couldn't afford to lose my cool at any step along this
journey. This whole ordeal was crazy-making, but I couldn't react
without losing ground. Anything I did that seemed like scribbling
outside the lines would count against me. I couldn't affect anything
anyway right now; I had to ride the snake and get through this
part of it. Then once I was in my cell, I could work on getting my
innocent black behind out of that hellhole... I felt a wave of terror

grip me at that thought. *My cell.* I was a whirlpool of emotions: fear, uncertainty, anger, outrage, righteous indignation, confusion... *Lord, please give me strength...!*

Dowis was still talking to the clerk when Officer Stinkeye shot me one last smirk and got up with his empty coffee cup in his hand. The door closed behind him—and I will never forget this—Dowis looked all around, leaned close to the clerk, and stated in a low voice, "Take care of him; he is a good one." He jerked his head toward me as he said it. The clerk smiled knowingly and nodded back. Well, that was unexpected—Dowis's remark had been a sympathetic appraisal after all. I figured that the police there thought like one living thing—but here were two officers who respected me as a man enough to slip me a little consideration in here. I knew I wasn't going to get five-star accommodations and a mint on my pillow, but that simple statement warmed my soul to no end. *"Take care of him; he is a good one."*

As fast as the props warmed me, a chill set in again. A good one or not, I was still walking into jail in handcuffs.

I looked at Officer Dowis, and as hard as it was for me to say this, it came out—and I said, "Thanks, man, I appreciate that." It felt unnatural to respond gratefully to a uniformed officer at the moment I was being persecuted by them, but giving the processing clerk the secret handshake like that for me was an overwhelming kindness. Now I will admit, I had to hold back a tear for two reasons. First, my emotions were running on overload. There had been a rising background level of tension throughout this case, and at this point it was threatening to explode. I was angry, frustrated, feeling betrayed—and I could not do anything about it. This was difficult for me, because throughout my life experiences and my training as a Marine, I have always been able to fight back. But the second reason that I held back that tear was because I knew where I was about to end up—somewhere a show of weakness was a signal to pile on, and I was not about to be punked by inmates or become someone's bitch. You know what I mean! I put on that hard "don't mess with me face," and quick. All of the premonitions I had felt about state prisons in the South was coming back to haunt me. Would I wind up down there, stuck behind bars in that miserable compound with my brains baking in the South Georgia sun? Would I end up in one of those chicken-house dormitories, locked up with thousands of hardcore psychos and vicious thugs? My guts were a snarl of anxiety. I felt like I was sinking in quicksand.

This was turning out not to be my day.

Then it happened: Electronic locks clicked, steel security doors opened, and I was processed into the system. What was going through my mind at this time was, "Now I'm a statistic." You know which statistic I'm talking about—the one that no proud black man ever wants to be part of: "*One out of every* [fill in the blank] *African American male has been arrested…*" I do not know what the current number is, but I do know I'm now part of that statistic—but the ironic thing is that I wasn't there for breaking the law. Far from it—I was doing my job to help an innocent woman whose life was on the line, and here I was being booked into jail for my efforts. I live a good, clean life. I worked hard to become the very picture of a solid citizen, and believe me, I am damned proud of that fact. But here I was, being pushed along and fingerprinted and photographed like any crack dealer or car thief. I looked around me at the glaring white-painted cinderblock walls in numb disbelief. I'd never even be seeing this place if I hadn't had the lousy luck of getting ensnared in the corrupt legal web of a bunch of mean-spirited power junkies. At that moment, I realized, I was as much as a puppet as Tonya Craft.

Looking back on this incident, I can trace the dividing line in my life. For me to be arrested this way opened my eyes to just how starry-eyed I have been, clinging to these boy scout ideals of what is right and honorable. This display of injustice has forever changed my view of the legal system. I knew I had done nothing wrong, and the legal system I have always admired, I admired no more.

So far throughout this book, I've shared my trip with you, and I've shown you things about myself. One of those things I showed you, my reader, was the turmoil in my mind when I had to interview that inmate at Valdosta State Prison. That was almost like foreshadowing that the interview I had there occurred before this happened to me. That visit to Valdosta had touched on deep-seated feelings I didn't know I had, and while those anxieties were still close to the surface, here they were being reawakened. To be frank, the idea of imprisonment freaked me the hell out. Perhaps that's one reason I toed the line all my life, this fear of having my autonomy utterly taken away from me. Being in the Marines was a different story—it wasn't so much a matter of taking my free will away from me as it was bulldozing down my old patterns and habits and then rebuilding a better person from the bare foundation up. But enduring prison time just tears a man's soul down; it doesn't create improved men but worse criminals. Upon seeing that bleak, miserable view of the Valdosta State Prison baking under a blistering sun, I had reflected then on how I never wanted to be on the other side of society's line—and here I was now, being treated like a criminal, just for trying to do the right thing. This was like a bad, bad dream.

My mind reeled back to July 2009, and the two hours of conversations I had had with Jerry McDonald. I looked at it from every angle, and I kept coming up blank. There was no force; I used no trickery or coercion. You've read for yourself the way it transpired through the transcripts of the audio recordings, and you can tell that the conversations I had with Jerry were conducted willingly on his part, in a friendly manner, and without threats. He wanted his side of the story to come out, and I was the one he chose to tell it to. And yet, here I was, arrested on three felony counts of influencing a witness.

The charges were as follow:

- Count One – Knowingly used threats toward Jerry McDonald with the intent to influence the testimony of said person in *The State of Georgia vs. Tonya Craft*, Catoosa County Superior Court Docket Number 2008-SU-CR-534
- Count Two – Knowingly used threats toward Jerry McDonald with the intent to induce [*his daughter's name*] to withhold testimony from *The State of Georgia vs. Tonya Craft*, Catoosa County Superior Court Docket Number 2008-SU-CR-534
- Count Three – Knowingly used threats toward Jerry McDonald with the intent to induce Kelli McDonald to withhold testimony from *The State of Georgia vs. Tonya Craft*, Catoosa County Superior Court Docket Number 2008-SU-CR-534

There it is, all in print. All my conversations were ONLY with Jerry McDonald. I never interviewed his wife Kelli or their daughter. It was just between us, and he wanted to talk. Where is the crime there? Are two American citizens not allowed to have a reasonable discussion if the powers-that-be decide it's against their personal interest? My goal, and Jerry McDonald's, too, when you get down to it, was the pursuit of justice

I have to admit, the arrest got me worried as hell. I said to myself, "*Arnt, you made your point.*" I talked to a few other private investigators and police officers I knew who had heard about my arrest, and they stated it was just a ploy from the district attorney to shut me up or slow down my investigation. But what really got me nervous was what took place December 9, 2009—the date I was indicted. When a case goes before the grand jury, that is serious. That meant the district attorney was going for a conviction, and on three felony counts. Each felony count means one to seven years in prison, so do the math—realistically I was facing somewhere from three to twenty-one years in prison for something I had not done. Now, I was worried, not only about my life, but about my family, and my fear and dread was making me rage at my oppressors, thinking of Arnt as a double-eyed son-of-a-bitch. But then, in the grips of my burning anger, I was reminded of one of the sermons my pastor had taught one Sunday morning. Pastor Bryan E. Crute of Destiny Metropolitan Worship Church is a major role model in my life, and his messages help mold me into the man I am today. The title of this particular sermon was "Attack Your Panic!" In this message, Pastor Crute spoke on a verse found in Romans:

"Dear friends, never take revenge. Leave that to the righteous anger of God. For the Scriptures say, '*I* will take revenge; *I* will pay them back,' says the Lord. Instead, 'If your enemies are hungry, feed them. If they are thirsty, give them something to drink. In doing this, you will heap burning coals of shame on their heads.' *Don't let evil conquer you, but conquer evil by doing good.*" [Romans 12:19-21 (NIV)]

I remember well Pastor Crute's message, and the spirit it is written in—the Holy Spirit. So when the time is right, I will be sending invitations for dinner and drinks to Chris Arnt, Alan Norton, Sandra Lamb, and Detective Deal—and if they refuse my invitations, I will send them each a gift card so they can have dinner on me.

## THE REAL REASON

Let me tell you the real reason why I was arrested. I would like to say it was because the district attorney was doing his job, or because Assistant District Attorney Alan Norton took an assigned case in which he truly believed a crime had been committed. But neither of these was the case. The real reason I was arrested was that Chris Arnt, Chief District Attorney for the Lookout Mountain Judicial Circuit, was pressured by political gain and financial influences. The District Attorney's Office wanted twenty-two guilty verdicts delivered against Tonya Craft so badly that they did whatever was in their power to attempt to secure those verdicts, including abusing that power—even if that meant arresting an innocent man. Arnt wanted to be a judge, and though he did not win in the election he ran in, he was going to make sure he had a feather in his cap the next time there was an election for judge, and that feather was Tonya Craft, strung up as a criminal for all to see. The financial influences in Catoosa County were the Lambs, the Newtons, and the Wilsons, all of whom disliked Tonya and had the power to control the District Attorney's Office. Pressure on the district attorneys (Franklin, Arnt, and Gregor) and on Judge House from those financial influences helped to create a network of lies, deceit, unethical behavior, and misconduct.

You see, the prosecuting district attorney knew that arresting me would prevent Tonya's defense team from having me testify in the case. And if the defense team did in fact put me on stand, then the prosecuting district attorney would portray me as a big, mean, black man who was going around Catoosa County threatening and intimidating the "good white folk." If I had taken the stand, all the district attorney would have had to do was ask me if I had been arrested and for what, and my answer would have had to have been: "Yes, for witness influencing." And then *whoosh*, I would have been out of there like there was a freaking trapdoor under the witness chair. Oh, they knew what they were doing, all right.

So I was left on the sidelines, unable to grab the ball and run it past the goal posts. But I wasn't sitting helplessly by. I was busy—I had my own legal case to prepare for, even as Tonya Craft's case was coming to trial.

Every member of the Craft defense team had worked like mad to get ready for the day that this case would see a courtroom. There was so much work to do to prepare for the trial that the time before it was like a ride in a roller coaster that wouldn't go fast enough—and the end of the ride was the unmovable brick wall of the trial date ... and, before the Tonya Craft team wanted to face it, April 12, 2011hit and it was time to lay our cards on the table, to put up or shut up, to fish or cut bait—pick your metaphor. However you say it, it was time to focus on the legal *mano á mano* that was going to decide the fate of a human being. The judge's gavel came down and signaled the start of *The State of Georgia v. Tonya Henke Craft.*

What with the regional aspect of the case and the small-town location of the trial, I hadn't expected press attention to be so intense—but the location of the events made its notoriety spread. Ringgold is in the center of a bullseye whose radiating circles touches multiple states: Catoosa County lies in the northwest corner of Georgia, on the Tennessee border, with Alabama smack up against them on one side, and the Carolinas not far off on the other. *Location, location, location...* The entire Tonya Craft trial was a news frenzy. A forest of white antenna masts sprouted up around the Catoosa County Justice Building as the media trucks converged. Both the Atlanta and Chattanooga television news outlets had teams covering the proceedings, along with newspeople from other large cities in the region and all of the national affiliate news crews. This strong media presence was in attendance at the courthouse throughout the entire trial. It was clear that this whole railroading Chris Arnt and Sandra Lamb had set up was going to play out in a very public way.

These representatives of the Fifth Estate were for the most part well-mannered and polite folks. The press conferences weren't like ones you'd see in a *Batman* movie scene with a huge, jostling crowd of news people on the steps of a stately government building (the ugly and depressing red-brick Catoosa County Justice Building was a poor stand-in for Gotham City Hall anyway). But like any crowd with a single driving purpose, when they sensed that something newsworthy and/or lurid was in the offing, they could swarm—and once you walk out a courthouse door to find almost a dozen microphones shoved in your face, it may as well be a hundred. But this case couldn't be ignored—"the Tonya Craft child molestation case," as the reporters exasperatingly insisted on calling it, had so many sensational elements to it. The daily events of the trial regularly headlined the local evening news, and all around the Central Southeast, break rooms, taverns, and coffee shops were abuzz with wild theories and heated arguments.

One reporter by the name of Melydia Clewell lit the spark that ignited the Craft case. She was an investigative reporter working with the NBC affiliate Channel 3 WRCB-TV in Chattanooga, Tennessee. When the first public reports of the Tonya Craft case reached outside of Ringgold, it was Melydia Clewell who aired it on the news. Melydia, also known on Twitter as "Nosie_Rosie," was at the trial every day, providing the public with a play-by-play account of what was going on in the court through frequent Tweeting. Limited to 144 characters or less, she developed shorthand. Replacing the word "question" with only the mark "?" was a handy touch; for defense attorney Demosthenes Lorandos, "D-Lo" became the accepted form. Every important development that occurred in that courtroom was sent to the outside world. I was grateful for the information, as I was kept far away from the trial, no thanks to Chris Arnt. After all my hard investigative work and the personal risks I took in service of my job, I was never able to take the stand on behalf of my investigation in the Tonya Craft case. As you can imagine, that drove me nuts. I felt like a ballplayer sidelined on the bench when my team needed me, but even after I got out of those handcuffs, my hands were still tied. I couldn't get near the place, but others did, and they kept me connected. I followed Melydia's Tweets, the chat room conversations, and William Anderson's blog reports, which informed me of trial developments on a daily basis.

Some of Melydia's courtroom Tweets, shown below, provided a running reference of the remarks Assistant District Attorney Len Gregor made about me and Tonya:

**FRIDAY, MAY 7, 2010 Updated 3:30 p.m.**

D-Lo objects to statements, ?s accusing Tonya of not wanting to talk to police. House allows it because topic raised during direct.

We are nearly 1 hour into cross-examination and haven't heard 1 ? about if Tonya molesting anyone.

Gregor painting a pic of going to hotel room w/investigator. Says, "a room with a bed, right?"

Gregor now moving to allegation she was spotted holding hands with her private investigator.

That being said, there was this one time in particular that I'm going to talk about here—because later, during Tonya's trial, District Attorney Len Gregor attempted to use this incident to inflame the jury.

It hadn't been enough for the prosecution to use my arrest to keep me from offering my evidence to the jury. As you have probably already figured out on your own from Melydia's Tweets, Assistant District Attorney Len Gregor had a further reason in keeping me out of that courtroom, as he showed in Tonya's cross-examination. He didn't want me to be able to contradict the crap—total *crap*—that spewed out of this man's mouth in a court of law. During the cross, ADA Len Gregor attempted to impugn Tonya Craft's character by insinuating that Tonya and I had an affair. He brought up the fact that the two of us had been seen together at a hotel—and then he pulled that leering *"with a bed, right?!"* line. I had no doubt he was drawing on the interviews the defense team had done at the hotel in Chattanooga, and as for hand-holding, hustling her out of that restaurant to avoid a scene over her ex would have explained that. But Gregor's love of left-field lowballing wasn't enough—he went even farther over the line. In a hushed courtroom, Gregor came out and said these words out loud:

*"If she could have an affair with a black man, then she could be a child molester."*

The jaw-dropping proclamation made by ADA Gregor was the most racist comment that I'm aware of anyone making in a courtroom in modern times. What was even worse, Judge Brian House did not raise an eyebrow about the comment! But plenty of other people noticed it, and they weren't about to keep quiet about it. And you know what? Neither am I. I was used as a pawn in their vicious little game, so I have a personal stake. And you know what else? Since Gregor played the race card in a forum he knew I was barred from, I'm going to invoke the same privilege. Now it's *my* turn to do a little racial profiling of the players in the Craft trial...

This statement was a transparent attempt by Len Gregor to inflame the jury, obviously hoping—expecting?—that the members of the jury were just as racist as somebody who could make a statement like that. Admittedly, it wasn't all that long ago that that sort of "reasoning" was business as usual in those parts. And Gregor was definitely appealing to that kind of mentality that would be enraged by such a suggestion. Catoosa County is about 95 percent white. The jury was all white; the judge and all of the attorneys were white; the alleged victims, white; all the witnesses, white; even the spectators in the courtroom were all white. I'm not making this racial—this is just stating the facts. Assistant District Attorney Len Gregor is the one who made it racial when he stated that if Mrs. Craft were sleeping with a "black man," then she could be a child molester. Gregor used me to inflame an all-white jury in a scene straight out of "To Kill a Mockingbird"—almost fifty blessed years after the book and the movie appeared! As I said, the district attorneys did and said whatever they wanted in order to secure twenty-two guilty verdicts against Tonya Craft, even to the point of playing such ugly dirty football. I have never heard of a more blatant display of trying to use race to secure a conviction in a criminal trial. With people like Gregor in the system, there is no wonder why there will always be racism and unfair justice in the legal system.

But Melydia Clewell wasn't the only reporter who was seeing past the prosecution's ham-handed ruse to inject a little sleaze into the proceedings. William Anderson, a dedicated judicial watchdog who was feeling increasingly outraged by the behavior of the prosecution in the Craft trial, also kept a steady stream of up-to-the-minute commentary on his blog. Anderson was familiar with my role in the Craft case and my own resulting legal tangle, and when District Attorney Len Gregor used me as a tool to derail justice, Anderson hit the ceiling. "How can they bring him up if they won't let him testify?" he wrote in one of his daily columns. DA Gregor's outrageous ploy of playing the race card to incite the all-white jury merited its own column, you can go to his blog to get the full entry, but below is part of William Anderson's report for Monday, May 17, 2010, titled "Eric Echols: Another Victim of the LMJC Prosecutorial Machine":

"Prosecutors who would do such a thing are people who will stop at nothing to get a conviction. This goes against every law and every ethical code in the State of Georgia, but so far Franklin, Chris Arnt, and Len Gregor have been allowed to run wild, smashing the law as they go.

"One might remember that Gregor, in his cross-examination of Ms. Craft, accused her of having a sexual affair with Mr. Echols. His proof? She had met him in a hotel room, and the room, Gregor astutely observed, has A BED. Thus, according to Gregor's twisted logic, if one is in the room with someone else and the room has a bed in it, then the people automatically have a sexual encounter. (The possibilities are endless, but I prefer not to go there.)

"Furthermore, because Mr. Echols is African-American, Gregor was trying to play a racial angle to inflame jurors by claiming Ms. Craft was SLEEPING WITH A BLACK MAN. This is something one might expect from a Scottsboro Boys Trial prosecutor, not someone in the year 2010, but there it is."

Good God! Even reading that now, a couple of years later, it still kills me. When I heard that "sleeping with a black man" accusation dragged into court, you bet I was mad, yeah—but mostly all I could do was shake my head in disbelief that they were pulling that ancient brand of backward-thinking prejudice. Hey, I'm realistic, if anything. I knew in that courtroom I was going to be cast as the heavy. Considering my serious professional demeanor and my Marine bearing—not to mention Sandra Lamb's calculating police report making me look like some kind of one-man urban assault force—it was practically a given that they would try to exploit the threat/intimidation angle.

But it wasn't enough for Arnt's team to paint me as a physical threat. They tried to suggest that I was a sexual threat—and the reason? Because I'm *black*—the implication being that I was an evil black man who had appeared there in their midst on a mission to tear down their polite, decent, God-fearing little white town. Oh yeah, right—as a polite, decent, God-fearing, churchgoing, married, home-owning, business-owning, taxpaying, respectable suburban professional, I'm a real menace to society, yo'! (Give me a break— and I *mean* that!)

You would think in a court of law that race could never be a factor—but it appalls me to have to add  that is still in the category of "just a little wishful thinking"! I find it difficult to accept that the prosecution thought that such low innuendo seemed like a smooth legal move to make, but this shows that even in our present day and age, someone can still think a tired ploy from back in the plantation days still has currency. As if all you have to do is just bring up an image of a black man and a white woman—and all of a sudden, *BOOM!* There's thunder on the soundtrack in some people's minds, and along with that thunder goes their logic—and once you've instilled that fear, then you can put anything over on them. I *swear...! Will it ever change?*

I'm sorry I'm going on about it like this— but you would not believe how tired I am of dealing with all of these lingering stereotyped clichés that go along with being black. Hell we all should be tired of it!.

Look, people, in case anyone has missed my message: *Will it ever change?* It's way past time to get with the program, because *the world <u>can</u> change.*

I know, it has been changing so fast that some of you might have missed it—but the main point is that yes, the world can *change.* And I know it's changed, because I've seen it changing with my own eyes and ears. I'm not that old—but it happened so fast that American society was still adapting itself as I was growing up.

It was as if our world began to grow a conscience and reformed an ugly side of its nature. To most people—thinking people—bigotry became an ugly mark of shame, a sign of ignorance. There's an expression for when the people get an idea and switch perspective—a "sea change." This sea change that the Civil Rights Movement brought was a tsunami, a cleansing wave. I mean, in the 1950's, who could have predicted that an imbalance that had existed for over a thousand years would be adjusted in just a couple of generations? That possibility is so unlikely that there must have been a divine hand in it. Because somehow the world changed within a single human lifetime—our entire society did a one-eighty from total segregation and sanctioned lynchings, to allowing all citizens equal justice under the law. All because the people—*we* the people, Americans of all colors and all religions—dared to see our world for what it was. The ideals upon which our country was founded, but there were ugly parts of it that needed to be changed, so we the people bound together to help it along, armed only with a dream that we could make the long-accepted ignorance end. And so, we the people went forward, dragging our society with us into that future to realize that dream, to make it shine here on earth. And in so many ways we have done that; we have changed our world...

...But despite all the high-sounding ideals, just thinking about how the world should be hasn't been nearly enough. There are parts of our world that still refuse to change. All of America's citizens haven't yet attained that sweet-sounding "equal justice under the law," because there are little pockets of people here and there who haven't got the wake-up call yet. And that just doesn't make sense—it makes me want to scream it to the skies: *Will it ever change?* It's infuriating that so much can change—but then fall just short of the goal. Here we've all come so far in reversing the attitudes of our culture, and then incidents like what happened to me in Catoosa County, Georgia, shine the light on places in the twenty-first century when ignorance is embraced and encouraged. You've read it with your own eyes here, from words printed in legal transcripts all there in black and white, the ways in which Catoosa County, Georgia, has proved itself to be one of those backward embarrassments.

In one fell swoop, Assistant District Attorney Len Gregor dragged enlightened thinking back into the closet and slammed the door shut on it. He tried to make it once again like the 1950s, where old scary stereotypes get waved around like a carnival horror show to whip up the audience, "to make the men act brave and ladies faint. I mean, come on! I'm not naïve, but all I'm going to say on this is "Will it ever change?"

I knew that this "sleeping with the black man" insinuation stemmed from the interviews conducted on September 27, 2008. I also knew that it was a sign of how low the prosecution was having to scrape in the absence of any hard evidence of wrongdoing. The scales of justice were at least looking like they had a chance of tipping in Tonya's favor. I was glad to have had a part in helping make her personal terror stop, because in reading the questions that Tonya's defense team asked of the prosecution's witnesses, I could tell that findings from my investigation were used. Later, after the dust had settled from the trial and the gag orders were lifted, Tonya Craft told me that if the defense team had felt at some point that I had been desperately needed to support any testimony, I would have been called, but the stakes were too high for the attorneys to call me as witness while I was still under an indictment charged with three felony counts. Bottom line, as a private investigator, my role was to do a proper and professional investigation and provide the facts I discovered to the client who hired me, and that's what I did—despite the efforts of twisted, bitter minds who wielded what turned out to be not much power at all.

# THE FINALE

After two years of investigations on Tonya's case, I must say this case was the most intense, consuming and demanding case I have ever been involved in. There were so many emotions in dealing with this case, some of which reached into my home. For Tonya, the criminal charges ended on May 11, 2010. It was a joyous day to be in the court and to hear the jury foremen voice ring out "not guilty" twenty-two times. Yes, I was very happy for Tonya and her family. Hell, I was happy for myself because I knew the work that The LPS Group, Inc., had put in on this case was a contributing factor to her acquittal.

In the meantime, my criminal case was progressing. In the eighteen months since my arrest, I had rejected three plea deals, one of which Assistant District Attorney Alan Norton presented for me to sign right before Tonya's trial. I was more than ready to have my day in court. I was looking forward to when I would be able to get the truth out at last. But before that could happen, in a startling move, all four judges in the Superior Court of Catoosa County—Wood, Van Pelt Jr., Graham, and House—recused themselves from hearing my case! Basically that meant none of Catoosa County Superior Court Judges wanted to sit on the bench and preside over my case. To me that was their way of saying "enough is enough". That recusal led to my indictment being quashed on November 17, 2010, on the grounds that the charges were "technically deficient." Another way of saying there were no merits to have secured an indictment. And then, on February 10, 2011, I received somewhat of a reward to this travesty I'd had to endure over the past two years.

As I was sitting at my desk looking over another case file, an email had come to my computer with a document attached, it was sent from Sam Sanders, my attorney. I opened it to see the engraved stationery of Herbert E. (Buzz) Franklin, district attorney of the Lookout Mountain Judicial Circuit. It was dated February 9, 2011, and had also been sent to the Honorable G. Grant Brantley, Chief Judge of Cobb County, Georgia, who wound up getting my case dropped in his lap when all of the judges in Catoosa recused themselves. Here are the contents of the notice:

**Re: State of Georgia v. Eric Dwight Echols, Catoosa County**

Dear Judge Brantley,

After reviewing the evidence and consultation with all interested parties, the State of Georgia has decided not to pursue further criminal charges in the above referenced matter.

Sincerely yours,
*[Signature of Alan Norton]*
Alan Norton
Assistant District Attorney

CC: The Honorable G. Grant Brantley
D.A. File 09CAT01261
Mr. Noah H. Pines
Mr. Samuel L. Sanders

Noah H. Pines of Ross & Pines, LLC, of Atlanta, Georgia, was the attorney I hired as part of my criminal defense. As I stated before, it's small wonder that I had lost my simple schoolboy belief in the justice system, especially in small towns. So it makes sense I'd want someone on my team who was not a part of backwater dealings. Noah Pines was that person.

As you can see, even the district attorney eventually came out and admitted his office had been wrong, that I never should have been arrested nor indicted. Yeah, I know I'm paraphrasing, since the letter sent to me stated only that there was insufficient evidence. So I ask you—can a person be arrested and indicted without evidence or witnesses? My answer is: Yes—if it's Catoosa County brand justice.

If you did not catch what I said, referring to the letter from the district attorney's office stating they were not proceeding with the charges. I stated "somewhat of a reward." How can a person such as myself—someone who has never broken the law, who has committed his life to his country as a US Marine, who has always helped others—how can I now feel that the letter from the district attorney was fully rewarding? I have dedicated my career to making a good, reputable name for myself in the field of security, loss prevention, and investigations. I have put in long, grueling hours with Fortune 500 companies to get noticed and promoted to executive-level positions. I was the first African American divisional vice president in loss prevention with Kmart. I was the first African American investigator and regional director in loss prevention with Lowe's Home Centers. My professional career in loss prevention and investigations was above reproach. Currently as a private investigator and as a certified minority business owner, I do business with top law firms and some fortune 500 companies. My creditability in this industry has always been high caliber, undoubting, and unwavering. My motivation behind The LPS Group, Inc., is to build a national family business that could provide for my family and theirs in years to come. But because I was once falsely arrested by the corrupt justice system of Catoosa County, the almost thirty years it took me to build my career and reputation was destroyed in a matter of hours.

From this day forward, if I have to take the stand as a witness in a case, if any compliance department conducts a check on The LPS Group to determine whether or not to award us a contract, and if I'm ever asked that question "Have you ever been arrested?" on a application to expand my business — now I am required by law to say, "Yes." My creditability is gone. My integrity has been taken away from me with words. The "yes" answer to that question will from this day forward put doubt in the minds of others. Let's be real, my file or application will go into that pile of those who answered yes to being arrested. Those of you that are responsible for hiring and approvals know this pile very well. And you know that pile takes longer for you to look at. This, people, is not right.

At the beginning of this book, I asked the question, "Will it ever change?" I'm talking about injustice and racial barriers, slurs, and prejudices. I told you earlier why I took this case, but the reason I stayed on this case was to do my part in correcting an injustice. In plain and simple terms, the thought of an innocent woman going to jail in a case I was assigned to investigate just did not sit well with me. Even when Tonya's funding ran out, we at The LPS Group, Inc., were the *only ones* who continued doing the work as if we were being paid. Yes, we were assured we would get paid later, and because of that assurance, we kept track of the hours and expenses worked on Tonya's case. Anyone in business as a private investigator or anyone who provides a legal service knows, if the client's funding runs out, the service stops.

But once things started turning ugly and the arrest happened, the personal stakes changed everything for me. My priorities shifted: the challenge of this case became not the investigation, but in showing that I could persevere. In the face of whatever they threw at me, I made it my main mission to prove that I could remain professional while continuing my job within a legal system that passed off corruption, deceit, and influence-peddling as justice. And once I saw the reactions of certain Catoosa County citizens to the fact that I'm black, the challenge became showing a predominately white community and all the people looking at this case that race should not play a part in justice, fairness, and helping an innocent woman. So those were the challenges that kept me going.

So I ask, "Will it ever change?" I pray that it will. Yes, I know God is almighty and can make the impossible possible, as I saw in the letter from ADA Norton when the charges against me were dropped. The district attorney had four years to reindict me, yet it was only three months from the time I received the order to quash the indictment to the time I received the letter about the charges being dropped. It pains me to think that our legal system is just another commodity that could be purchased, traded or bartered and justice is based on who you are and who you know. In an area where the truth is to be upheld and revered, it's not only sadly ironic—it's an outrage that perverts the very foundations upon which our justice system is built. My goal was the pursuit of justice—and despite the efforts of the alleged purveyors of justice in Catoosa County, justice was served, in both my case and

Tonya's. Man, that must piss some people off to no end. And the thing that kills me is that with this big public mirror held up to them, they've had a chance to see their own behavior and their petty vindictiveness exposed—and they still probably don't feel that they've done anything wrong.

But they did do something wrong, and it was exposed to the light of day.

August 28, 1963 is a date you all should remember. On this date, during the march on Washington, D.C., one of the most remembered speeches in our nation's history was heard from the steps of the Lincoln Memorial. There, standing on the steps of this great American monument before a crowd estimated at almost three hundred thousand souls both black and white, one of our nation's heroes and the leader of the American Civil Rights Movement, Dr. Martin Luther King Jr., spoke for seventeen minutes. His powerful, righteous voice rang through the National Mall, reaching the ears of the hundreds of thousands gathered there and the untold millions more gathered around their radios and televisions—the ringing words of his "I Have a Dream" speech. Many people have analyzed this speech, trying to read layers of secret meanings into Dr. King's stirring words. Some claim that when Dr. King stated "this nation will rise up," it hints at a revolution between whites and blacks; and that when Dr. King intones, "One day, on the red hills of Georgia…" that the red symbolizes the blood, the pain, the struggles and the injustice that blacks endured. To me, this speech dealt with Dr. King's dream of attaining equal jobs and equal freedom for blacks. It was his vision and prayer that we as a people can all get along as brothers and sisters no matter of our race or religion, that every American has the same civil liberties and rights as the next person. The most remembered part of this speech for me, which still to this day should be heard from every mountaintop, is: "Let freedom ring."

Dr. King stated:

*"Let freedom ring from Stone Mountain of Georgia.*

*Let freedom ring from Lookout Mountain of Tennessee.*

*Let freedom ring from every hill and molehill of Mississippi.*

*From every mountainside, let freedom ring.*

*And when this happens, when we allow freedom ring, when we let it ring from every village and every hamlet, from every state and every city, we will be able to speed up that day when* all *of God's children, black men and white men, Jews and Gentiles, Protestants and Catholics, will be able to join hands and sing in the words of the old Negro spiritual:*

*Free at last! Free at last!*

*Thank God Almighty, we are free at last!"*

I write these words in August of 2011. Two years ago this month, I was arrested by the Catoosa County sheriff. Forty-six years ago in the same month of August, Dr. Martin Luther King Jr. paused in his speech to look out across a sea of humanity and, his voice echoing through the hearts of a nation, stated the words: "Let freedom ring from Lookout Mountain of Tennessee." The fact that the name of the judicial system that falsely arrested me was the Lookout Mountain Judicial Circuit is and sought for three felony convictions. So, "Will it ever change?"—the selective withholding of justice, the unethical behavior by those in power to obtain political gain, and the oppression of blacks? Can't we at least shake off the last vestiges of this lingering racism? I don't believe it will ever change, at least not in my lifetime.

There is a great quote from Henry David Thoreau which states, "Things do not change; we change." But people, even as a nation, don't all change just like *snap*—even when it's obviously time for new ideas, dreams, and concepts to be regarded, accepted, and embraced. Sometimes these changes that are so perfect and logical and welcome still must be fought for at great cost. The sad fact remains that despite our best intentions, even after the social conscience of a civilization has turned a corner, not all of the human crowd turns that corner at the same time.

My grandparents even my parents, were witness to the two extremes of the human condition. They had grown up in a time when they or their older relatives could still trace the scarred outlines cut into wrists and ankles from cruel iron shackles; they saw that with their own eyes. And then, with those same eyes, they saw firsthand the tremendous change in American society when the Civil Rights Act was passed. Dr. King's dream began to happen so fast that it was really like a dream, as if the whole world got up to march together hand in hand, through blood and fear and hate, to the other side into a new dawn—a dawn whose light, sadly, has yet to reach parts of the world. Fifty years later, the changes that should have been effected by the civil rights legislation of the sixties is still struggling to move forward in places like Catoosa County, where people choose to remain in a self-imposed limbo of ignorance.

I know all too well that what I exposed in Catoosa County isn't the dying embers of the last burning cross. But I showed it for what it was, an ugly blight on the human spirit. The ugliness was so striking—in Tonya's case, literally—that it threatened to overwhelm the fact that there are good people in Catoosa County.

I thank God for the people I met along my way who helped counter the skewed impression I was getting of that part of the country. They were like the antidote to a poison, truly they were. Like the Tonya Craft supporters, who to my flattered surprise became Eric Echols supporters—which is a good term, supporters, because they were exactly that. They held up my sagging spirits throughout this ordeal.

Those concerned citizens, sick in their guts of seeing justice perverted day by day, who used the internet to speak out and air the truth—I can't thank them enough for getting involved in this whole messy fight. I'm grateful for the technology we have, because it turned an eye on both Tonya Craft's and my situations, but it also enabled the word to spread and, most importantly, questions to be asked. It was like that chant from the Sixties: "The whole world is watching." Thanks to our electronic age, while this action was set on a tiny stage in Ringgold, Georgia, the whole world really could look in, if it wished. It's like the future is realizing its power when something as simple and tiny as a camera phone can be held high like Liberty's torch!

But more than anyone, there's one person who proved to me that this place had somewhat of a heartbeat, because his is so revealing: Jerry McDonald, a man who dared to put the truth above the mob mentality when his basic nature told him to just go with the flow. He could have just gone along with that whole scripted witch hunt and let that legal trapdoor open under my feet. But *he* knew otherwise, and he couldn't just let it go because doing the right thing was hard-wired in him. Ultimately, it was Jerry McDonald who had the backbone to break ranks and say no to a hateful scheme and its despicable lies.

Jerry's example reaffirmed some of my faith in people. It gave me hope that there might be more people like him out there in these backward places, thinking people who will see the bad old wrongs still existing among themselves and stick their necks out enough to do something about it. It's almost a *yes* answer to my echoing question: "Will it ever change?" Only because Jerry McDonald never had to speak with me for two hours and Jerry McDonald told the District Attorney he was not testifying against me on those false felony charges they cooked up.

But I still have to say—no, not by a long shot. It's not just Catoosa County; racially motivated injustice is something that's still endemic in our society at every level. But people know that it's wrong, and where it exists, it's sneaky and hidden. I mean, in this day and age, you sure don't see such heinous race baiting openly used as a gimmick by the power elite in a court of law. I was a lightning rod that exposed how this old-school form of franchised racism still lingers, even now. The grassroots backlash that rose up as a result shows that when the people have a say in it, by and large, they resent letting that backward mindset represent their community as the standard. But I don't want to give the impression that it's all a big, happy love-in. Sure, mankind took a giant leap—but when you think about where we *can* be, we fell short. There's still too far to go to say the battle is won just yet.

But Tonya Craft won her battle—at the cost of hundreds of thousands in legal fees, plus her children, her career, her house, her life...and her soul. I'm sure she must feel like some part of it's been stolen away. Afterward, you can't go on the same way, not once you know that someone out there could hate you, I mean really *hate* you so damn much that they could smile in your face while doing something so monumentally evil to you... Knowing that sort of pointless vindictiveness is out there takes something away. You begin to mistrust the world the way it mistrusted you. You're too afraid to not watch your back. Someone made your life hell, but you're free of it—yet you're in a prison anyway. They manage to win even when they lose.

I take one last look around before I take my leave of Catoosa County. The twister damage is like a visual shorthand for what they've gone through here; this place has been torn apart twice over. I reflect that it tore my life apart, too—and one day I will forgive as I'm a forgiving man. I hope this land can heal itself, in so many ways. I pray that all the people here can come around. I've seen that there's goodness here, and promise—but if a promise isn't acted upon, it's nothing but a hollow lie. And Catoosa County has about choked to death on lies already.

I get in my car and pull out. The broken pine trees give way to solid forest as I head on down the highway. I look in the rearview mirror, but already I can't tell anything was even there.

In this enlightened day and age, what happened to me is hard to dismiss. What this means to me is that even though I am an upright American citizen in so many ways—I'm a proud black man, I'm a proud Marine who served his country, I own a business, I love and cherish my wife, I pay my taxes, and I have a lovely, well-kept home in a nice neighborhood—even with all that to my credit, to some people, I will never exist as a man before they see my color. I will always just be black or like Sandra Lamb spat out, "a black bastard." Wherever this is a mindset, it is a cancer that rots the whole social system from within. Those people who serve in our justice system are in place to protect the law—but when they are the ones violating the law, or even worse fabricating evidence to prosecute the innocent, that mindset shows us where the sickness lies. There will never be a change until the mindset of people as a whole change. And in the face of that impossibility, the constant thing that is good and honest and right must be our justice system. The light of truth must be steady and unwavering. To any American suffering an injustice, that's the light that guides us through the dark night to the end of the tunnel.

The good parts of our history are where ideas changed for the better, and most of us are aiming for the next challenges in a new century. It's time for the last stragglers in the crowd to turn that corner. Fifty years is more than long enough to catch up with the rest of the world.

I ask you...

*Will it ever change?*

"And he said: 'I tell you the truth, unless you change and become like little children, you will never enter the kingdom of heaven.'" Matthew 18:3 (NIV)

I am Eric D. Echols, Private Investigator and this is my story.

Made in United States
North Haven, CT
09 January 2022

14416911R00143